PEOPLE of COMPASSION

Dave Andrews

WIPF & STOCK · Eugene, Oregon

Wipf and Stock Publishers
199 W 8th Ave, Suite 3
Eugene, OR 97401

People of Compassion
By Andrews, Dave and Marshall, Anne
Copyright©2008 by Andrews, Dave
ISBN 13: 978-1-61097-855-2
Publication date 2/1/2012
Previously published by TEAR Australia, 2008

THE BE-ATTITUDES

[3] Blessed are the poor in spirit,
for theirs is the kingdom of heaven.

[4] Blessed are those who mourn,
for they will be comforted.

[5] Blessed are the meek,
for they will inherit the earth.

[6] Blessed are those who hunger and thirst for righteousness,
for they will be filled.

[7] Blessed are the merciful,
for they will be shown mercy.

[8] Blessed are the pure in heart,
for they will see God.

[9] Blessed are the peacemakers,
for they will be called children of God.

[10] Blessed are those who are persecuted because of righteousness,
for theirs is the kingdom of heaven.

Matthew 5:3–10

Who are the people of compassion blessed in the be-attitudes?

1. The poor — or poor in spirit — who identify with the poor 'in spirit'.
2. Those who mourn — who grieve over the injustice in the world.
3. The meek — who get angry, but who never get aggressive.
4. Those who hunger and thirst for righteousness — who seek justice.
5. The merciful — who are compassionate to everyone in need.
6. The pure in heart — who are whole-hearted in desire to do right.
7. The peacemakers — who work for peace in a world at war.
8. Those persecuted for righteousness — who suffer for just causes.

If we were to use the virtues blessed in the be-attitudes as guidelines for our lives, what kind of people do you imagine we would be?

1. We'd identify with the poor 'in spirit' *(humility)*.
2. We'd grieve over injustice in the world *(empathy)*.
3. We'd get angry, but never get aggressive *(self-restraint)*.
4. We'd seek to do justice, even to our enemies *(righteousness)*.
5. We'd extend compassion to all those in need *(mercy)*.
6. We'd act with integrity, not just for the publicity *(integrity)*.
7. We'd work for peace in the midst of the violence *(non-violence)*.
8. We'd suffer ourselves, rather than inflict suffering *(perseverance)*.

When reading *People of Compassion*, ask yourself these questions:

» Which of the be-attitudes is embodied best in the story you have just read?
» What can you learn from this story about embodying this attitude in your life?

CONTENTS

INTRODUCTION TO DAVE ANDREWS FOR THE 2012 DAVE ANDREWS LEGACY SERIES

INTRODUCTION .... *I*

TELEMACHUS *The Mad Monk* *3*

NICHOLAS *The Man Who Was Santa* *5*

MARTIN OF TOURS *A Soldier for Christ* *7*

BASIL OF CAESAREA *The Good Bishop* *10*

PATRICK *The Patron Saint of Slaves* *13*

BENEDICT *A Gentle Guide for Beginners* *16*

AIDAN *An Apostle of Charity to the Barbarians* *19*

WENCESLAUS *The Good King* *22*

HUGH OF LINCOLN *The Hammer of Kings* *25*

FRANCIS OF ASSISI *God's Juggler* *27*

ELISABETH OF THURINGIA *The Queen Who Served Beggars* ... *30*

NILUS SORSKY *A Voice in the Wilderness* *33*

MENNO SIMONS *The Architect of the Pacifist Faith Communities* ... *36*

GEORGE FOX *A Witness Against All Violence* *39*

NIKOLAUS LUDWIG *The Count Who Cared* *42*

JOHN WESLEY *The Whole World Is My Parish* *45*

CHARLES FINNEY *Christ's Lawyer* *47*

SOJOURNER TRUTH *'Ain't I A Woman?'* *50*

CAROLINE CHISHOLM *A Woman's Woman* *53*

TE WHITI *The Forgotten Forerunner of Non-violent Resistance* ... *56*

FLORENCE NIGHTINGALE *The Lady of the Lamp*	*59*
HENRI DUNANT *Founder of the Red Cross*	*62*
JOSEPH DE VEUSTER *Damien the Leper*	*65*
MARY MACKILLOP *A Fair Dinkum Aussie Saint*	*68*
JOHN GRIBBLE *'The Black Fellow's Friend'*	*71*
PANDITA RAMABAI *The Learned One*	*74*
C.F. ANDREWS *Christ's Faithful Apostle*	*76*
HELEN KELLER *The Light in the Darkness*	*80*
TOYOHIKO KAGAWA *Love-Intoxicated Personality*	*83*
DOROTHY DAY *The Woman Who Wanted To Change The World*	*86*
ALBERT LUTHULI *The Apartheid Opponent*	*90*
DIETRICH BONHOEFFER *The Man Who Stood By God*	*93*
SIMONE WEIL *'The Red Virgin'*	*96*
DOM HELDER CAMARA *'The Red Bishop'*	*98*
PASTOR SON *The Man Who Adopted His Enemy*	*101*
JACQUES ELLUL *The Prophet Of Bordeaux*	*103*
CLARENCE JORDAN *The Race-Mixing Communist*	*106*
JOSÉ MARIA ARIZMENDIARRIETA *The Co-op Priest*	*108*
DESMOND TUTU *The Voice of the Voiceless*	*110*
GLADYS STAINES *A Widow Shows The Way Forward*	*113*
REFERENCES	*116*

*Life would be almost unbearable
without such people,
I think it would be unbearable.
They are the people who say by their lives
that human life is valuable —
that my life is valuable —
and that there is a reason for living.
Without them, history would just be
one horror after another.*

—Thomas Cahill, author of
How the Irish Saved Civilisation and
The Gifts of the Jews

Introduction to Dave Andrews for the 2012 Dave Andrews Legacy Series

I KEPT SEEING THIS guy on the shuttle bus - long hair, graying beard, a gentle 60's-70's feel to him. He seemed thoughtful, intense, friendly, and quiet, like he had a lot on his mind, as did I. Even though I saw him nearly every time I boarded the shuttle bus, we didn't speak beyond him smiling and saying, "G'day" and me nodding and saying, "Hey" as we boarded or disembarked.

It was my first time at Greenbelt, a huge festival about faith, art, and justice held every August in the UK. I had always heard great things about the event and so was thrilled when I was invited to speak. I was just as thrilled to get a chance to hear in person some musicians and speakers I had only heard about from a distance, so I went through the program and marked people I wanted to be sure not to miss.

It was near the end of the conference when a friend told me to be sure to catch an Australian fellow named Dave Andrews. "I've never heard of him," I said. "Oh, he's a force of nature," my friend said. "Kind of like Jim Wallis, Tony Campolo, and Mother Teresa rolled up into one." How could I not put a combination like that in one of the last free slots on my schedule?

I arrived at the venue a few minutes late and there he was, the bearded guy from the bus. Thoughtful, intense, and friendly, yes — but *quiet* he was not. He was nearly exploding with passion — passion and compassion, in a voice that ranged from fortissimo to fortississimo to furioso. How could a guy churning with so much hope, love, anger, energy, faith, fury, and curiosity have been so quiet and unassuming on the bus?

He was a force of nature indeed, evoking from his audience laughter, shouts, amens, reverent silence, and even tears before he was done. He spoke of justice, of poverty, of oppression, of solidarity across religious differences, of service, of hope, of celebration, of the way of Jesus.

As I listened, I wanted to kick myself. *This is the most inspiring talk I've heard at this whole festival. Why did I miss all those opportunities to get to know this fellow on the bus? Now the festival is almost over and I've missed my chance!*

Later than evening, I boarded the shuttle bus for the last ride back to my hotel, and there sat Dave and his wife, Ange. I didn't miss my chance this time. I introduced myself and they reciprocated warmly.

I was a largely unknown American author at the time and hardly known at Greenbelt, much less in Australia, so I'm quite certain Dave and Ange had never heard of me. But they couldn't have been kinder, and as we disembarked, he pulled two books from his backpack and told me they were a gift.

The next day when I flew home from Heathrow, I devoured them both on the plane. First, I opened *Not Religion, But Love* and read it through from cover to cover. Then I opened *Christi-anarchy* and couldn't put it down either. When my plane landed, I felt I had been on a spiritual retreat . . . or maybe better said, in a kind of spiritual boot camp!

Things I was thinking but had been afraid to say out loud Dave was saying boldly and confidently. Ideas I was very tentatively considering he had already been living with for years. Complaints and concerns I only shared in highly guarded situations he was publishing from the housetops. Hopes and ideals I didn't dare to express he celebrated without embarrassment.

I think I gave him a copy of one or two of my books as well, and I guess he was favorably impressed enough that we stayed in touch and a friendship developed. I discovered that we were both songwriters as well as writers, that we both had a deep interest in interfaith friendships, that we both had some critics and we both had known the pain of labeling and rejection.

Since then, whatever he has written, I've been sure to read . . . knowing that he speaks to my soul in a way that nobody else does.

We've managed to get together several times since our initial meeting in England, in spite of the fact that we live on opposite sides of the planet. We've spoken together at a few conferences on both hemispheres, and I had the privilege of visiting him in Brisbane. I've seen the beautiful things he has been doing in a particularly interesting and challenging neighborhood there, walking the streets with him, meeting his friends, sensing his love for that place and those people. He's been in my home in the US as well, and we've been conspiring for some other chances to be and work together in the future.

In my speaking across North America, I frequently refer to Dave's work, but until now, his books have been hard to come by. That's why I'm thrilled to introduce this volume to everyone I can in North America.

Yes, you'll find he's one part Tony Campolo, one part Jim Wallis, and one part Mother Teresa, a force of nature, as I was told.

You'll also find he is a serious student of the Bible and a serious theological sage — the kind of reflective activist or thinker-practitioner that we need more of.

In a book like *Christi-anarchy*, he can boldly and provocatively unsettle you and challenge you. Then in a book like *Plan Be*, he can gently and pastorally encourage and inspire you. Like the central inspiration of his life, he is the kind of person to confidently turn over tables in the Temple one minute and then humbly defend a shamed and abused woman from her accusers the next.

You'll see in Dave's writings that he is highly knowledgeable about poverty, ecology, psychology, sociology, politics, and economics . . . not only from an academic standpoint, but also from a grass-roots, experiential level. His writing on these subjects grows from what he has done on the ground . . . for example, nurturing a community network that is training young adults to live and serve among the poor, supervising homes for adults who are learning to live with physical and psychiatric disabilities, encouraging small businesses to hire people who others would consider unemployable and developing a non-profit solar energy co-op for local people.

Dave's writings and friendship have meant so much to me. I consider him a friend and mentor. Now I am so happy that people across North America can discover him too.

You'll feel as I did - so grateful that you didn't miss the chance to learn from this one-of-a-kind, un-categorizable, un-containable, wild wonder from Down Under named Dave Andrews.

Brian D. McLaren
author/speaker/activist (brianmclaren.net)

INTRODUCTION

Most of us struggle to be the very best we can be. And for many of us, Jesus Christ of Nazareth represents the very best that we — as human beings — can ever hope to be.

It might be too much to expect to have Christlike abilities. Few, if any of us, could calm a storm, or raise the dead. But it's not too much to expect to be more Christlike in terms of our sensibility. Now, more than ever, we need to learn to care for people like Christ did.

Fortunately, the path of Christlike compassion is one that others have trodden before us, and their lives can serve as examples.

Thomas Cahill says, 'Life would be almost unbearable without such people, I think it would be unbearable. They are the people who say by their lives that human life is valuable — that my life is valuable — and that there is a reason for living. Without them, history would just be one horror after another.'[1]

I don't think it helps us to treat anyone as *saints*. To hold people up as models of sinless perfection, when they're not, doesn't help them or us. *Halos* only create delusions of grandeur that become reasons for discouragement when disillusionment eventually sets in.

The relevance of the *example* of others before us depends on our remembering and reconsidering them as they were — *imperfect people in relentless pursuit of the practice of perfect compassion.*

These stories first saw the light of day in *Target Magazine*, a publication of TEAR Australia, a Christian aid agency for which I work. The early stories were edited by Steve Bradbury and the later ones by Lyn Jackson. The images were sourced — painstakingly — by Di Jeffs and recreated brilliantly by Anne Marshall. Thanks to Chris Bradbury for her meticulous proof-reading. Hugh Todd was the designer.

In telling these stories I have tried to be accurate. But because they are sketches — outlines, not portraits — details are missing. For a full picture you need to read their biographies and autobiographies yourself!

Dave Andrews, Brisbane, Australia

[1] In Anita McSorely, *The St. Patrick You Never Knew*, St. Anthony Messenger, March 1997.

TELEMACHUS

The Mad Monk

Telemachus was born in the fourth century after the birth of Christ. He lived as a monk in a remote Asiatic Christian community, growing vegetables and studying prayer.

Then one day, in prayer, Telemachus sensed that the Spirit was encouraging him to leave his community and go to Rome, which at that time was like the capital of the world, a big bustling metropolis at the centre of the greatest empire the world had ever known. When Telemachus arrived in the so-called 'heavenly city', Rome was celebrating a recent victory of its powerful legions over the troublesome Goths, and so, for the holiday festival, a circus was being staged for the jubilant multitudes. Telemachus didn't know where he was going, but he allowed himself to be swept along by the crowds on their way to the Colosseum for the circus.

When the crowds arrived at the Colosseum, they began to get excited at the sound of the lions roaring their challenge and the gladiators preparing for combat. Telemachus didn't know what was happening, but he followed the crowd into the Colosseum where, to his horror, he was confronted with callous, gut-wrenching carnage, as gladiators fought one another to the death, slaughtering their hapless foes without pity, as a red-blooded entertainment for the blood-thirsty crowds.

It was all too much for Telemachus.

He felt that he had to do something. He simply couldn't stand by idly and do nothing while human beings were being beheaded, disembowelled, and dismembered before his very eyes. So Telemachus ran down the steps of the stands, leapt into the arena, and began darting back and forth between the fighters, crying, 'Forbear! Forbear! In the name of Christ I beg you to forbear.' When the crowd saw the scrawny figure of the monk, running frantically about the arena, ducking and weaving between the combatants, they took Telemachus to be a bit of welcome comic relief, and roared their approval. But as time went by, some of the people in the crowd began to hear what 'the mad monk' was saying, and, as more and more of the crowd came to realise that Telemachus was actually trying to spoil their bloody fun, they turned against him, hissing and booing, and bellowing at the top of their voices for his quick despatch.

What happened next, no one seems to know for sure. We do know that the gladiators lunged at the monk with thrusts of their swords; and we do know that the audience buried the monk under a hailstorm of stones. But we do not know whether it was the gladiators or the audience that killed him. All that we know is that, when the furor was over, Telemachus lay dead in the middle of the arena.

Then a strange thing happened.

In the silence that ensued, it was as if the monk's last cry echoed eerily around the arena once again: 'Forbear! Forbear! In the name of Christ I beg you to forbear.' Overcome with shame, the spectators departed, leaving the circus empty. Never again did spectators gather to watch people butcher each other at the Colosseum in Rome. All brutal gladitorial battles were banned. And Telemachus was written into the pages of history as the hero who, single-handedly, brought the era of slaughter as entertainment to an end.

It is probable that the declining power of the empire, resulting in diminishing numbers of recruits for gladitorial schools, and decreasing amounts of funds available to stage gladitorial contests, were also very significant factors in putting an end to the circus; but Telemachus will always be remembered as the man who, in the end, was actually prepared to put his body on the line to stop the slaughter.

> *'Forbear! Forbear! In the name of Christ I beg you to forbear.'*
> *— Telemachus*

Suggestions for Meditation
» What aspect of this story did you relate to most?
» Which be-attitude do you feel Telemachus embodied best?
» What is the most valuable lesson you can learn from this story?

Remember Jesus said:
'Greater love has no one than this,
that they lay down their life for their friends.' *John 15:13*

NICHOLAS

The Man Who Was Santa

Colin can't wait to play Santa. He has already started growing a long white beard to go with his long white hair. Each week he gets up at church and begs for donations from the congregation. He claps his hands with delight at the prospect of distributing these presents as gifts to kids at Christmas time.

Julian is Colin's friend. He likes Colin. But he hates Santa. Talk to Julian about Santa, and as quick as a flash he'll tell you that 'Santa' is an anagram of 'Satan'. Julian says the fat guy in the red suit with a fake smile is nothing but a corporate-sponsored point man flagging the start of our annual Yuletide consumerfest.

Colin and Julian represent two very different views of Santa. Colin is closer to the Dutch tradition, which celebrates *Sinterklaas*. Julian is closer to the German tradition that, at one point, banned Santa Claus.

To the Dutch, Santa was a mythical figure who hailed from Spain, with a Moorish helper called Black Peter. He had the amazing capacity for knowing, without saying, whether children had been bad or good throughout the year. And he rewarded good children generously with sweets that mysteriously appeared in their shoes in midwinter.

To the German reformers, Santa was a silly fiction who had become a serious problem, because he had begun to displace Christ at Christmas, the very festival held in his honour. The reformers tried to deal with the problem by banning Santa and focusing on the *Christkindlein* or the Christchild.

As it turned out, it wasn't long before *Christkindlein* evolved into *Kristkingle,* or 'Kriss Kringle', who, as time went by, came to look more and more like Santa Claus.

In spite of the prohibition, Santa Claus would not be denied his day of fun. 'Santa Claus' is a corruption of Saint Nicholas. In the fourth century, Nicholas was the Bishop of Myra, a city in Lycia, in southwestern Turkey. Apparently, Myra was an important port of call for the many ships plying their trade round the Mediterranean Sea.

During a famine, Nicholas is said to have stolen grain from the cargo of a passing ship that had stopped at Myra on its way from Egypt to Byzantium. He distributed the food freely to all the hungry citizens of the city, thus saving the town from starvation.

On another occasion, Nicholas is said to have heard about the plight of a poor family in Myra with three daughters, but no money for their dowry. In those days, a woman without a dowry was unlikely to be able to arrange a suitable marriage, and without the support of a family was likely to end up on the streets.

So Nicholas decided to provide them with their dowries himself. According to the story, wanting to avoid publicity, Nicholas, under the cover of darkness, slipped some gold into the stockings the girls had washed in the evening and had hung out overnight to dry. In this way, the sisters were saved from prostitution.

> *'The story of the bishop does more for me than the antics of many of the buffoons that bear his name!'*
> — Dave Andrews

The date of his birth is unknown, and the date of his death is still uncertain, but Nicholas is thought to have died on December 6, either in 345 or 352AD. When the story of what Nicholas had done became known, the bishop was named a saint; and the legend of Saint Nicholas, or Santa Claus, the gift-giving saint, was born.

I must confess that the story of the bishop does a lot more for me than the antics of many of the buffoons that bear his name!

Suggestions for Meditation:
» What aspect of this story did you relate to most?
» Which be-attitude do you feel Nicholas embodied best?
» What is the most valuable lesson you can learn from this story?

Remember Jesus said:
'Freely you have received, freely give.' *Matthew 10:8*

MARTIN OF TOURS

A Soldier for Christ

Martin was born about 316AD in Hungary. His father was a tribune in the Imperial Horse Guard of the Roman Army, and he named his son after Mars, the god of war.

Martin showed an interest in Christianity from an early age, but his father was suspicious of the 'sect' and discouraged his son. However, against his father's wishes, ten-year-old Martin begged to be a *catechumen* or candidate for baptism. In contemplative prayer, the young Martin found the spirituality he was looking for.

At the time, sons of veterans had to serve in the Roman Army. So, at fifteen, Martin was forced to join the military. He refused to co-operate. He was put in chains until he promised to take the orders he was given. He was then assigned to a cavalry unit. While in the army, Martin tried to live like a monk rather than a soldier. As an officer, he was entitled to a servant, but he switched roles with his servant, cleaning the servant's boots instead of the other way around.

Around 334AD, Martin was sent as an officer to do garrison duty in Gaul (now France). On one bitter winter day, while Martin was riding towards the gates of Amiens, he came across a ragged beggar, freezing and half-naked in the cold. Overcome with compassion, he took off his warm lambswool officer's cloak, slashed it in two with his sword, wrapped one half of it round the beggar and draped the other half around his own shoulders. That night, Martin dreamt that he saw Jesus wearing the half of the cloak he had given to the beggar, and heard Jesus saying to the saints around him: 'Look at this cloak! Martin the *catechumen* gave it to me!' When he awoke, Martin went and got baptised straight away. But it would be two more years before Martin could leave the legion and follow his vocation.

In the meantime, Martin struggled with the conflicting demands of trying to live as a 'soldier of Christ' in a Roman Legion. When the Franks invaded the northern borders of the empire, Martin refused to fight, saying: 'Put me in the front of the army, without weapons or armour; but I will not draw sword again. I am become the soldier of Christ.' His commander was more than happy to grant this request, and put him in prison until he could be sent to the front. Fortunately, the Franks sued for peace, and Martin was discharged from the army.

Martin left his legion and went to the city of Tours where he was mentored by Hilary of Poitiers. He encouraged Martin to set up a monastery in Marmoutier near Tours. Here, 80 people lived simply and communally. 'Most of them were clothed in garments of camels' hair. Any dress approaching to softness was deemed criminal. No one there had anything which was called his own; all things were possessed in common.' (Sulpicius Severus)

> *'Put me in the front of the army, without weapons or armour; but I will not draw sword again. I am become the soldier of Christ.'*
> — Martin of Tours

Martin's monastery became a key instrument of mission in Gaul. He used it as a base from which he travelled, visiting villages and humbly sharing the gospel. Wherever people responded, Martin formed them into faith communities under the guidance of a monk. 'Before Martin, very few in those regions had received the name of Christ; but through his example that name has prevailed to such an extent there is no place which is not filled with very crowded churches.'

Martin impressed people all over Gaul with his manner. According to one witness, Martin 'judged none and condemned none. No one ever saw him angry or annoyed. He was always the same, and presented to everyone a joy of countenance.' It is not surprising that in 371AD, Martin was made Bishop of Tours. As Bishop, Martin used his position both to vigorously advocate the faith, and to actively defend the rights of dissenters who disagreed with the church on matters of faith.

Priscillian, a Spanish theologian, was one whom Martin defended. Priscillian taught that, in order to be the Bride of Christ, people should renounce marriage and practise mysticism. The Bishops of Spain, no doubt as much disturbed by Priscillian's denunciation of their ambition as anything else, brought charges of practising magic against him at the Imperial Court. Martin rushed to plead Priscillian's case before the Emperor Magnus Maximus. After listening to Martin, the Emperor relented and decided not to use civil power to enforce church polity. But after Martin returned home, the Spanish Bishops persuaded the Emperor to behead Priscillian, along with all his supporters. Thus in 385AD, the first executions of Christians by fellow Christians took place.

As soon as Martin heard about the executions, he hurried back to the Imperial Court. He publicly denounced the Bishops and refused to share the sacraments with them. The Emperor, fearing escalating conflict, said he'd show mercy to the supporters of the former Emperor, if Martin would show mercy to the Bishops. Martin agreed, but regretted it deeply. He boycotted assemblies of Bishops until his death.

Martin died when he was over 80 years old. He was buried, at his request, in the Cemetery of the Poor.

Suggestions for Meditation:
» What aspect of this story did you relate to most?
» Which be-attitude do you feel Martin embodied best?
» What is the most valuable lesson you can learn from this story?

Remember Jesus said:

'I am sending you out like lambs among wolves.' *Luke 10:3*

BASIL OF CAESAREA

The Good Bishop

Basil was born the second of ten children in about 330AD in Caesarea, Cappadocia (Asia Minor). His father was a devout man, whose family property had been confiscated when they stood up for their faith during an earlier period of intense persecution. Later, the family had been able to restore their family fortune. Despite their wealth, Basil's parents lived very frugally, giving money to mission, helping the poor and providing hospitality to strangers.

Because he struggled with his health, Basil's family took him to live at his grandmother Macrina's estate. She taught the young Basil about their family's faith. As he grew older, his father, a famous lawyer and teacher, took charge of Basil's education 'in virtue' himself. His father died when Basil was fifteen, and he was sent back to Caesarea to complete his education. There, he met Gregory of Nazianzus, a fellow student who was about the same age and from a similar background.

In about 349AD, Basil went to Constantinople and then Athens to study philosophy. Gregory of Nazianzus was already there. The two students from Cappadocia loved speculation and disputation, and became firm friends. Both were serious about their studies, discouraging their fellow students from attending Bacchanalian banquets, and encouraging them to engage in thoughtful Christian philosophical reflection.

Basil believed that reflection should be active, not merely academic. He returned home, to be confronted by some profoundly significant challenges in his own family. Basil's sister's husband had died, and his sister Macrina (named after his grandmother) had decided not to re-marry, but live a life of piety and charity in service of the poor. His younger brother, Naucratius, had decided to do the same, supporting a number of elderly people by fishing and hunting. Sadly, he drowned in a boating accident. In the light of these examples, Basil decided to abandon his career and follow in their footsteps. In 356AD, he marked this complete change in his life's direction by being baptised.

In 357AD, after visiting monasteries in Mesopotamia, Palestine, Syria and Egypt to see how other committed Christians were living 'alternative Christian lifestyles', Basil joined Macrina and their mother in setting up their own intentional Christian community household at Annesi. Here, Basil and his brother Gregory — called Gregory of

Nyssa—invited Basil's friend Gregory of Nazianzus to join them. The three became great friends.

At that time, there was a great theological dispute in the church about the nature of God, and the three friends argued for the idea of God as 'three-in-one'. At the Council of Constantinople, Basil suggested God should be understood as a community — 'one substance (*ousia*) and three persons (*hypostasies*)' — a concept now accepted as orthodox trinitarian doctrine.

Basil wrote two famous ethical texts — the *Moralia* and *Regulae*. The former provided guidelines for life in society in general, and the latter provided guidance for life in monasteries in particular. Basil emphasised the importance of monasteries being communities, rather than collections of solitaries. He advocated that all monasteries should serve the poor in their localities, requiring all prospective members to sell at least some of their property to give to the poor. He saw the core business of monasteries as embodying the love of God in the flesh.

> *'The bread which you use is the bread of the hungry; the garment hanging in your wardrobe is the garment of him who is naked; the shoes you do not wear are the shoes of the one who is barefoot; the acts of charity that you do not perform are so many injustices that you commit.'*
> — Liturgy of Saint Basil, 373AD

In 370AD, he was made the Bishop of Caesarea after Bishop Eusebius died. Basil used his position as a platform to denounce 'simony' (making money from religious activities) and 'usury' (making a profit from the poor by charging interest on loans), and to encourage the support of people suffering from drought and famine.

Basil's health was never very good. He died in 379AD, before he was 50. During his short but significant life, his influence had been so great that people began to refer to him as 'Basil the Great'. The title stuck.

A lasting monument to his care for the poor was the great institute before the gates of Caesarea, which was used as a poorhouse, hospital and hospice.

Suggestions for Meditation:
» What aspect of this story did you relate to most?
» Which be-attitude do you feel Basil embodied best?
» What is the most valuable lesson you can learn from this story?

Remember Jesus said:
'May they be one — as we are one.' *John 17:11*

PATRICK

The Patron Saint of Slaves

Patrick was born in Bannevem, a village in Roman-occupied Britain, in 386AD. His family were wealthy Roman citizens. As Christians, they gave their son a Christian name — Patricius. However, Patrick took very little interest in Christianity.

When he was 16, Patrick was captured by Irish raiders and, along with many thousands of others, taken back to Ireland and sold as a slave. There he was put to work as a herder on the hills near Ballymena. During that time, Patrick learnt the Celtic language and, through his master, a Druid priest, learnt Druid customs.

Patrick resented his enslavement and rebelled against it with every fibre of his being. But he said that, in the atmosphere in which he found himself, 'the Spirit was glowing' and 'the Lord opened my unbelieving eyes.' In that context, Patrick began to see the possibility of developing a Christian faith beyond the bounds of Greco-Roman civilisation. He envisaged a Judeo-Christian religion which, like the Hebrew tradition before it, would picture 'the world as holy, as a Book of God — fraught with divine messages', and which could thus embrace creation, and sensation, with gratitude and joy, rather than anxiety and guilt.

When he was 22, Patrick had a vision in which he was told: 'Look, your ship is ready. You are going home.' So Patrick escaped, made his way through 200 miles of hostile territory to the sea, and jumped aboard a ship. He fled to the Continent, where he spent some time at the Monastery of St Martin at Marmoutier. He then entered the religious life at Lerins, before returning home to Britain to spend time with his family.

While he was back in Britain, Patrick had another vision in which he was called to return to Ireland. In this vision, he saw Victoricus, a man that he knew in Ireland. Victoricus handed Patrick a letter entitled 'The Voice of the Irish'. When he read it, Patrick said that he heard a whole multitude of voices calling to him, saying 'Holy boy, we beg you to come and walk with us once more.' This dream became the defining call on Patrick's life. It reoccurred time and again, calling him to 'walk with' the Irish. As he said later, his vocation was not to civilize them, or to convert them, but to walk humbly alongside them, as one of them.

In 419AD, Patrick returned to Europe to prepare for his mission to

Ireland. For 12 years, Patrick, who was painfully aware of his lack of formal education, studied hard to prepare himself. In 431AD, when Palladius (the first missionary bishop sent to Ireland) died, Patrick was sent to take his place. In 432AD, Patrick landed at Saul, where he stayed during the winter. In the spring, Patrick traveled to Tara, which he set up as his base of operations. From there, Patrick and his friends made trips to all parts of the region — Meath, Leitrim, Cavan and West Ireland — preaching, teaching, and opening schools and churches. Wherever he went, Patrick would leave some of his closest friends to consolidate the work that he had started.

> *'I came to the Irish people to preach the Gospel and endure the taunts of unbelievers, putting up with reproaches about my earthly pilgrimage, suffering many persecutions, even bondage, and losing my birthright of freedom for the benefit of others.'*
> —Patrick

Patrick had a keen pastoral concern for people. He challenged the princes to modify their traditional laws in the light of the gospel. He advocated that the laws be codified, and that all people be equal before the law. Some princes whom Patrick discipled moderated the adverse impacts of tax laws on the poor through law reform.

Patrick was concerned with women as well as men. According to Thomas Cahill, Patrick was 'the first male Christian since Jesus to speak well of women.' Patrick spoke of women as 'true adults — blessed, noble, beautiful' — 'who follow Christ with backbone' in spite of the 'menacing and terrorizing they endure'. He was particularly concerned about the plight of women who were kept in slavery.

Understandably, Patrick took a strong stand against slavery. In his famous 'Letter to the Soldiers of Coriticus', Patrick protested about the slave trading done by these Celts. Patrick's letter is remarkable for two reasons: firstly, because it is the first authentic document of the Celtic church; and secondly, because it is the first church document anywhere to condemn slavery in all its forms.

Patrick died in 460AD. He was the first person in recorded human history to speak out unequivocally against slavery. It would take nearly another 1500 years before the UN Universal Declaration of Human Rights condemned it.

From the Confession of Saint Patrick

Patrick's Prayer
Christ be with me, Christ within me,
Christ behind me, Christ before me,
Christ beneath me, Christ above me,
Christ beside me, Christ to win me,
Christ to comfort me and restore me,
Christ in quiet, Christ in danger,
Christ in hearts of all that love me,
Christ in mouth of friend and stranger.

Suggestions for Meditation:
» What aspect of this story did you relate to most?
» Which be-attitude do you feel Patrick embodied best?
» What is the most valuable lesson you can learn from this story?

Remember Jesus said:
'I no longer call you servants.
Instead, I have called you friends.' *John 15:15*

BENEDICT

A Gentle Guide for Beginners

Benedict was born into a noble Roman family at Nursia in Italy in 480AD. In Rome, he went to school, pursuing literary studies. At the age of 19 or 20, he became convinced that, if he was reading the Gospels correctly, he should 'forsake' his family's wealth, set aside his academic career, and 'serve only God'.

Benedict left the city, and moved to Enfide in the Simbrucini mountains about sixty kilometres outside of Rome. There he joined 'a company of virtuous men'. While he was with them, Benedict's understanding of spirituality was radically transformed. He was convinced that preaching 'good news to the poor' demanded grass-roots, hands-on solidarity with them.

While on the way from Enfide to Subiaco, Benedict met a monk by the name of Romanus. Romanus talked with Benedict about his spiritual journey, advising the noble's son that the best way for him to move on to the next stage of his journey towards simplicity would be to take a monk's habit and live as a hermit in a nearby cave. Benedict jumped at the chance to empty himself of his pride and live in simple humility.

Over the next three years, Benedict lived alone, with a growing reputation for wisdom among the locals who sought his counsel from time to time. When the abbot of a nearby monastery died, the monks begged Benedict to become their leader. He declined, knowing their reputation as a quarrelsome community. But they persisted, and Benedict eventually became their abbot. The experiment proved to be a complete disaster. The monastery was more troublesome than Benedict had imagined it would be. The monks even tried to poison him. So Benedict retreated to his cave once again.

Benedict's painful experience caused him to think about the nature of Christian community. Over the years, he developed what he called a 'little rule for beginners' in Christian community — a 100-page primer that later became known as the 'Rule of St Benedict'. The word 'Rule' may sound harsh to our ears, but Benedict was determined to make sure there was 'nothing harsh' in his primer.

Benedict's Rule was not written just for monks and nuns, but for every person who wanted to practise the love of Christ in their ordinary, everyday life. It encouraged people 'in all things' — whether waking or sleeping, eating or drinking, studying or working — to 'take care of things'.

Benedict was convinced that the best way for people to learn to 'take care of things' was in a Christian community which encouraged a balance between individual responsibility and relational accountability. His Rule was intended to serve as a simple, practical guide to a healthy, holy, communal way of life for the members of the thirteen small Christian communities that Benedict slowly built up round Subiaco.

'Let all guests that come be received as Christ.' — Rule, 53

Benedict believed that the dynamics at the heart of a healthy, holy, communal way of life were *work* and *prayer*. He said people could not 'take care of things' unless they were prepared to work hard. They were unlikely to be prepared to work hard unless their work was suffused with prayer, because for nobles to voluntarily do manual labour alongside serfs was a revolutionary idea at the time.

Benedict did not prescribe a particular type of work. He expected people to take up any work that was required. It was not *what* was done, so much as *how* it was done, that counted. Everything was to be done in a way that would care for others — 'relieve the poor, clothe the naked, visit the sick, help the afflicted, bury the dead' (Rule, 4) — and so demonstrate their love for Christ. 'Let all guests that come be received as Christ' (Rule, 53). 'Let the sick be served in deed as Christ Himself' (Rule, 36).

In his Rule, Benedict said that for any community to be really viable, it needed stability and order. To enhance stability, Benedict encouraged people to commit themselves to a particular community for life. To ensure order, Benedict encouraged the people in a community to elect their own abbot and to then submit themselves to his leadership — with the proviso that every abbot's decisions would be subject to public scrutiny and to open debate by all the members of the community on all matters of importance.

Benedict's advice to an abbot was clear and direct. 'It beseemeth the abbot to be ever doing some good for his brethren, rather than to be presiding over them. He must be sober and merciful, ever preferring mercy to justice, that he himself may obtain mercy. Let him keep his own frailty ever before his eyes, and remember that the bruised reed must not be broken. Let him study rather to be loved than feared' (Rule, 64).

Benedict died in 543AD. He didn't know it at the time, but his 'little rule for beginners' — embodying ideas of 'a written constitution, an elected authority limited by law and the right of the ruled to review the legality of the actions of their rulers' — would become a critical catalyst for the development of 'due process'.

Suggestions for Meditation:
» What aspect of this story did you relate to most?
» Which be-attitude do you feel Benedict embodied best?
» What is the most valuable lesson you can learn from this story?

Remember Jesus said:
'Everything that I learned…
 I have made known to you.'
John 15:15

AIDAN

An Apostle of Charity to the Barbarians

Aidan was probably born in Connacht, Ireland. He studied with the saintly Bishop Senan on Scattery Island, in County Clare, to become a monk. He joined the monastery on the island of Iona in Scotland, where Oswald of Northumbria, the second son of an English king, had been living in exile as a refugee since 616AD.

The Britons had become Christians when Britain was part of the Roman Empire. Later, the faith had been taken beyond the boundaries of the Empire to Ireland by people like Patrick. With the collapse of the Roman Empire, the Angles from Germany invaded Britain and drove back the Britons, and English chieftains like Aethelfrith established their pagan kingdoms all over Britain.

The English chieftains often fought with each other and, in the course of battle, Aethelfrith was killed. His children fled from northern England to south-west Scotland in search of sanctuary. They found it at a monastery on the island of Iona. The Irish monks welcomed these English refugees, and gave them the protection and support they needed. Through the kindness of the monks, Oswald developed a deep commitment to Christ.

In 633AD, Oswald made a triumphant return to Northumbria and re-established himself as king. Once his position was secure, Oswald sent a message back to Iona for some help in evangelising his people. The first person sent to help Oswald was Corman, but he found the English difficult to work with, and returned to Iona where he declared the Angles to be of an 'obstinate and barbarous temperament'.

Aidan suggested that perhaps the problem was not the English, but the evangelist. He said that, based on what he heard, Corman had been 'unreasonably harsh with his unlearned listeners'. The monks concluded that the empathy Aidan showed for the English was a sign that he was the right man for the job, and sent him to replace Corman as their missionary to the Angles of Northumbria.

Aidan arrived in Northumbria in 635AD. He set up his base on an island called Lindisfarne or the Holy Isle. Lindisfarne was isolated and protected — the perfect place for a monastery. It had a causeway connecting it to the mainland, which appeared twice a day at low tide, so the monks could travel back and forth on their missionary journeys.

Aidan established an Irish-style monastery of round huts, a communal meeting place and a small church. The monks developed a routine of prayer and study. In preparation for their mission trips among the English, the Irish monks invested a lot of time in learning the English language. Oswald not only helped the monks learn the language, but also accompanied them on their trips as an interpreter.

Aidan's approach to mission was simple. He walked round the countryside and chatted with the people whom he met along the way. Where people showed some interest, Aidan sent his monks to regularly visit their villages and form small local Christian communities. Aidan was so committed to the importance of walking and talking with people, that when the king gave him a horse to help him on his travels, Aidan promptly gave the prize steed to the next beggar he met who asked for alms. The king, by all reports, was furious that Aidan had given away this expensive gift. But Aidan reprimanded him, saying that as far as he was concerned, people were more important than presents.

> *'He and his followers lived as they taught — namely a life of peace and charity.'* — Venerable Bede

Not surprisingly, Aidan developed a great reputation among the English for his integrity and generosity. According to witnesses, Aidan was 'indifferent to the dignity of a bishop, but influencing all men by his humility'. He 'delighted in distributing to the poor whatever was given him by the rich men of the world'. Aidan used the gifts of money he was given to ransom people sold into slavery.

The Venerable Bede, a staunch critic of Celtic Christianity, gladly acknowledged that 'the highest recommendation of (Aidan's) teaching to all was that he and his followers lived as they taught'. Bede specifically noted Aidan's qualities that he admired most: 'his love of peace and charity; his chastity and humility; his mind superior to anger and avarice, and despising pride and vain glory; his industry in keeping and teaching the heavenly commandments; his diligence in reading and watching; his authority becoming a priest in reproving the haughty and powerful, and, at the same time, his tenderness in comforting the afflicted and relieving and defending the poor...he took care to omit none of all those things which he found enjoined in the apostolic writings, but to the utmost of his power endeavoured to perform them all in his actions.'

Aidan died in 651AD. Bede says that as a result of Aidan's consistent witness 'many Northumbrians, both noble and simple, laid aside their weapons, preferring to take monastic vows rather than study the art of war...He and his followers lived as they taught — namely a life of peace and charity...'

Suggestions for Meditation:
- » What aspect of this story did you relate to most?
- » Which be-attitude do you feel Aidan embodied best?
- » What is the most valuable lesson you can learn from this story?

Remember Jesus said:

'Be as shrewd as snakes and as harmless as doves.' *Matthew 10:16*

WENCESLAUS

The Good King

Wenceslas, or Wenceslaus, as he was called, was born into the royal family of Bohemia in the year 903AD. When his father died in 924AD, Wenceslaus, at the age of twenty-one, became Duke of Bohemia.

The first thing Wenceslaus did when he became King was to put an end to the bloody war between Bohemia and Germany. Wenceslaus did this by taking the risk of personally seeking reconciliation with Emperor Henry of Germany. And the alliance Wenceslaus achieved finally brought some peace to his beloved Bohemia.

Later, when the peace broke down, and fighting flared up again along the borders, to save his soldiers from being slaughtered by a much bigger and much better equipped army, the King offered to settle the matter by fighting a duel, one on one, with a powerful opposing General.

As they prepared for mortal combat, apparently the General found himself struck down by a strange attack of paralysis and he was forced to concede victory in the contest to the King.

Typically, Wenceslaus forgave the enemy chief, and spared his life on the condition that he withdrew all his forces from Bohemian soil immediately.

During the period of peace that ensued, Wenceslaus redirected the energy and resources usually committed to the war effort to reconstruct the infrastructure of the country.

He sought to reform the legal system and brought about many measures to establish social justice. He instituted freedom of religion. He set prisoners free who were unfairly imprisoned. He abolished torture as a form of punishment.

And he tore down the gallows, laden with the corpses of criminals, that dotted the countryside.

At the same time, Wenceslaus personally extended his hospitality to strangers, provided rations for the poor, and guaranteed protection for the widows and orphans in his care.

It's hardly surprising that the people loved 'Good King Wenceslaus'. But the aristocracy, whose arbitrary authority he threatened, hated him with a vengeance. They took their vengeance out on him in 935AD when they assassinated Wenceslaus, at the age of thirty-two, in an ambush organised by the nobles and led by his brother, Bolislaw.

As he lay dying, Wenceslaus said to Bolislaw: 'May God forgive you.'

Bob Adams says: 'Young King Wenceslaus, who we sing about at Christmas time, was a hero whose humane ideas were very much ahead of his time.'

Perhaps, in some respects, he still is.

Good King Wenceslaus

Good King Wenceslaus looked out, on the Feast of Stephen,
When the snow lay round about, deep and crisp and even.
Brightly shone the moon that night, though the frost was cruel,
When a poor man came in sight, gathering winter fuel.

'Hither Page, and stand by me. If thou knowest, telling,
Yonder peasant, who is he, where and what his dwelling?'
'Sire, he lives a good league hence, underneath the mountain,
Right against the forest fence, by St. Agnes' fountain.'

'Bring me flesh and bring me wine, bring me pine logs hither.
Thou and I shall see him dine, when we bear them thither.'
Page and Monarch, forth they went, forth they went together,
Through the rude wind's wild lament and the bitter weather.

'Sire, the night is darker now, and the wind grows stronger.
Fails my heart. I know not how. I can go no longer.
'Mark my footsteps good, my Page. Tread thou in them boldly.
Thou shalt feel the winter's rage, freeze thy blood less coldly.'

In his master's steps he trod, where the snow lay dinted.
Heat was in the very sod, which the saint had printed.
Therefore faithful folk be sure, wealth or rank possessing,
Ye who now would bless the poor, shall yourselves find blessing.

Suggestions for Meditation:
- What aspect of this story did you relate to most?
- Which be-attitude do you feel Wenceslaus embodied best?
- What is the most valuable lesson you can learn from this story?

Remember Jesus said:

'The good shepherd lays down his life for the sheep.'

John 10:11

HUGH OF LINCOLN

The Hammer of Kings

Hugh, though regarded as an English saint, was born in France, in 1140. The family that he came from had a reputation for compassion. Anne, his mother, used to tend to the needs of the lepers in her community, literally washing the feet of those whom no-one else even wanted to touch. Not surprisingly, growing up under the guidance of his mother, Hugh began to develop a very practical, compassionate spirituality himself.

When he was old enough, Hugh decided to join the Carthusians. The Carthusians were part of a monastic reform movement that was seeking to get back to the essentials of the gospel. In the Carthusian monastery at Grande Chartreuse, Hugh was appointed the procurator, entrusted with the care of the guests, and as such it was his responsibility to take care of the poor who flocked to the monastery for help.

Hugh's reputation as a hardworking helper of the poor began to spread far beyond the borders of his native France. And it wasn't too long before Henry II invited Hugh to come to England to set up a monastery in Somerset. Hugh said he would be more than happy to comply with Henry's request; but only on the condition that the King would compensate the peasants, whose land he had apparently already compulsorily acquired for the project!

In 1186, the popular Prior was appointed Bishop of Lincoln, a diocese that stretched from the Humber River in the north to the Thames River in the south. Hugh arrived in Lincoln accompanied by a splendid cavalcade of canons and knights, humbly dressed as a simple monk, riding astride a mule. He walked barefoot to the Cathedral for his investiture, and afterwards threw a great party for the poor of the city, assuring them that from then on, one third of all episcopal revenues would be set aside for their welfare.

Hugh began to reorganise the diocese — rebuilding the Cathedral that had been damaged in an earthquake; and founding a School of Theology at the Cathedral that became a famous centre of religious learning. Hugh not only visited the poor, but also invited them to his home. Like his mother before him, he would wash them, kiss them, and send them on their way with a gift. Hugh didn't claim to be able to heal them. Rather, he said 'It is my soul that the leper heals with a kiss!'

When Henry died, Richard became King of England, and the 'Lion Heart' embarked on a series of Crusades. During the Crusades, violence against the Jews erupted all over England. Hugh acted quickly to intervene on behalf of the Jews. He not only offered them refuge in the Cathedral, but also personally stood between them and the armed mobs that were out to get them. Thus Hugh saved the Jews of Lincoln from the terrible massacre that engulfed the Jews of York.

> *'I leave everything I appear to possess to our Lord Jesus Christ in the person of the poor.'*
> —Hugh of Lincoln

Hugh, unlike most clergy, refused to support the King's foreign military adventures in any way, and refused to pay any war taxes—the first recorded case of conscientious tax objection in history! The King threatened to confiscate the Church's property, and the Bishop threatened to excommunicate anyone who tried. The King was furious, but the Bishop held firm, leading John of Leicester to call Hugh of Lincoln 'The Hammer Of Kings!'

Hugh died on 16 November in the year 1200. On his death bed he declared he never possessed anything; but lest the Treasury confiscate the property he had at his disposal, Hugh said, 'I leave everything I appear to possess to our Lord Jesus Christ in the person of the poor'.

Suggestions for Meditation:
» What aspect of this story did you relate to most?
» Which be-attitude do you feel Hugh embodied best?
» What is the most valuable lesson you can learn from this story?

Remember Jesus said:
'I am the gate for the sheep;
whoever enters through me will be saved.'
John 10:8

FRANCIS OF ASSISI

God's Juggler

Giovanni was born in Italy in 1182. His father changed his name to Francesco after a trip to France. And the 'little Frenchman' was brought up on romantic French ballads sung by travelling troubadours.

The son of a wealthy merchant, Francesco Bernadone led a cavalier life in Assisi until, in his early twenties, he fought in a battle against a neighbouring town, was captured and incarcerated. This was to prove a turning point for Francesco.

Following his release Francesco gave away his horse, his armour, and his weapons. His father, exasperated over Francesco's prodigality with family property, organised a meeting with the bishop to pull his son into line. But it backfired.

Francesco renounced his family, and his family's property, altogether. He gave back everything his family had given him, including the clothes he was wearing at the time. Francesco stood there naked as the day that he was born.

Then he turned to his father and said: 'Until now I have called you father, but from now on I can say without reserve, 'Our Father who is in Heaven' — I place my confidence in Him.'

Francesco decided to spend some time living as a hermit beside an old church in San Damiano. While there, Francesco heard a voice saying, 'Rebuild my church'. Francesco responded by repairing the ruins of the church in San Damiano, then set about the task of reforming the life of the church throughout Italy.

Francesco approached the task of renewal — not as a legislator — but as a juggler! He aspired to be like one of the jugglers who accompanied the troubadours, drawing the crowds, so they could listen to the music of the heart the musicians played. As Le Jongleur de Dieu (a 'Juggler for God'), Francesco wanted to travel from town to town like an entertainer, without a penny to his name, introducing people to *joie de vivre* (the 'true joy of living').

Thousands of people responded. And Francesco pointed them to the Sermon on the Mount as the simple gospel imperative. For he longed for them to model the life of Jesus in the world.

Remarkably, considering his views, Francesco did not rage against the opulence of medieval society. Ever the romantic, he tried to woo people away from the trappings of power, and get them to fall in love with the lovely 'Lady Poverty'. For him, poverty was not an end in itself. People needed to joyfully embrace poverty in order to follow Jesus.

In 1210, Francesco obtained approval from Pope Innocent III for a simple rule dedicated to 'apostolic poverty'. He called the order the 'Friars Minor', and this band of 'Little Brothers' followed the example of their founder in caring for the poor.

In 1212, Clare — a wealthy friend from Assisi who, like Francesco, had given all her wealth to the poor — started a sister order to the brothers, known as 'the Poor Clares'.

At this time, many Christians understood mission in terms of crusades – slaughtering as many Muslims as they could — in the name of the Lord. Francesco not only refused to take up weapons himself, but travelled to Egypt where the crusaders were fighting, and begged them to lay down their swords.

When they wouldn't listen to him, Francesco crossed the lines at Damietta, to talk with the 'enemy' sultan, Mele-el-Khamil, telling him about the 'Prince of Peace', and trying to broker a peace deal 'in His name'.

While Francesco was overseas, disputes arose among the Friars. A Vicar-General was appointed to take control of the order, and a new set of rules were instituted which changed the character of the movement.

Francesco retired to a hermitage on Monte Alvernia — where the man we know as St. Francis died in 1226.

> Lord, make me an instrument of thy peace.
> Where there is hatred, let me sow love;
> Where there is injury, pardon;
> Where there is doubt, faith;
> Where there is despair, hope;
> Where there is darkness, light;
> Where there is sadness, joy.
> O Divine Master,
> Grant that I
> may not so much seek
> To be consoled, as to console;
> Not so much to be understood, as to understand;
> Not so much to be loved as to love;

For it is in giving that we receive;
It is in pardoning that we are pardoned;
And it is in dying that we are raised to eternal life.
— *Francis*

Suggestions for Meditation:

» What aspect of this story did you relate to most?
» Which be-attitude do you feel Francis embodied best?
» What is the most valuable lesson you can learn from this story?

Remember Jesus said:

'Give to the one who asks you,
and do not turn away from the one who wants to borrow from you.'
Matthew 5:42

ELISABETH OF THURINGIA

The Queen Who Served Beggars

Elisabeth was born in 1207 in Thuringia, the daughter of King Andrew II and Queen Gertrude of Hungary. King Andrew II was, by all reports, a bad king, whose misrule led his nobles to a revolt against him. His wife Queen Gertrude was apparently a good woman who, unfortunately, became implicated in the politics of the day, and was assassinated by the nobles in 1213. Elisabeth was just seven years old when her mother died. But before she died, Gertrude managed to do two things that were to shape the rest of her daughter's life.

The first thing was to share her faith with her daughter. Gertrude was a very devout Christian, and she encouraged Elisabeth, from a young age, to pray regularly.

The second thing was to arrange her daughter's marriage. By the age of two, according to the custom of the time, Elisabeth was betrothed to the eldest son of a local noble. When this son (Herman) died, she was betrothed to the second son, Ludwig.

Ludwig married Elisabeth in 1221, when he was 21 and she was 14. 'Piety, Chastity, Justice' became their family motto. They committed themselves as a couple to pray regularly, practise hospitality, and rule justly.

In the same year Ludwig and Elisabeth were married, the Franciscans set up their first base in Germany. Brother Rodeger, one of the first German Franciscans, became Elisabeth's spiritual mentor. He encouraged her to live out the Franciscan ideals of kindness and service as much as she could.

Elisabeth was very rich, and brought a large dowry into her marriage with Ludwig. She had so many castles, she was called 'Elisabeth of Many Castles'. But as time went by, this wealthy woman became increasingly concerned for the poor. She began to ride around the countryside, assessing the plight of the impoverished.

Elisabeth couldn't see the need and not respond to it. She began distributing alms all over the kingdom, even giving away the robes of state and the ornaments of office. But Elisabeth didn't stop at charity. She looked for ways to give herself. She built a 28-bed hospital for the poor in Wartburg, and visited the patients daily. She herself helped feed 900 hungry people each day.

Ludwig and Elisabeth lived such exemplary lives that people started to refer to them as 'St Ludwig and St Elisabeth'. They were not only exemplary, they were also happy, with three children — Hermann, Sophia and Gertrude.

Then, in 1227, Elisabeth's beloved husband, Ludwig IV, died. The 20-year-old Elisabeth was inconsolable. 'The world and all its joys are now dead to me,' she cried. The next year, Elisabeth sent her children to stay with her aunt, formally 'renounced the world', gave away her inheritance, and joined the Franciscans as the first lay member of the order in Hungary.

The queen now dedicated herself to serving beggars, providing them with clothes, shoes and agricultural tools. She opened the first orphanage in eastern Europe for destitute children. And, at the hospice she established in Marburg, she tended to the needs of dying lepers with her own hands, washing the sick and burying the dead.

> *'Elisabeth...took the elements of her personal responsibility, set out tantalisingly in the New Testament, and imagined a social model which... would change our societies.'*
> — John Ralston Saul

On 17 November 1231, Elisabeth died, worn out as much by the lack of support from her spiritual director as from her implacable service to the poor. However, at the age of 24, she was one of the most influential activists in 13th century Europe.

The political philosopher, John Ralston Saul, says of Elisabeth: 'She and Francis of Assisi were the most famous activists of their day. To a great extent, they laid out the modern democratic model of inclusion — an important step towards egalitarianism. Elisabeth used her position...to put the ideas into action.

'Like many others, she created a hospice. But unlike others, she went beyond pity and charity...It is hard to imagine now the public impact of a royal figure washing the bodies of the homeless dead. Imagine the Prime Minister, or the Governor General for that matter, not just visiting or holding hands with street people, but actually washing their bodies for burial.

'Elisabeth...took the elements of her personal responsibility, set out tantalizingly in the New Testament, and imagined a social model which...would change our societies.'

Suggestions for Meditation:
- What aspect of this story did you relate to most?
- Which be-attitude do you feel Elisabeth embodied best?
- What is the most valuable lesson you can learn from this story?

Remember Jesus said:

'I have washed your feet; you also should wash one another's feet.'
John 13:14–15

NILUS SORSKY

A Voice in the Wilderness

Nilus Sorsky was born in Russia in 1443. At an early age Nilus, named after an early church father, joined the famous Russian Orthodox monastery of St. Cyril of Belozersk at White Lake.

Very sincere about his faith, Nilus quickly became disillusioned with the corruption in the White Lake monastery. So, as an able scholar, he obtained permission to study at the revered Russian Orthodox monastery on the Holy Mountain of Athos in Greece.

Nilus made the most of this time at Mount Athos. He was particularly interested in the traditional practice of Christ-centred contemplative prayer as a discipline of the heart. Nilus also studied the early church fathers. He wrote: 'I lived like a bee flitting from one fine flower to another in order to know the garden of life'. Nilus was particularly drawn to the writings of Basil of Caesarea and his ideas about intentional Christian community. He took every opportunity he could to visit other monasteries round the Mediterranean, looking for communities based on the ideas of the early church fathers.

On his return to Russia, he had to stay at the White Lake monastery for a while, but as soon as he could, he moved as far away as possible. He found a place in a swampy region of wilderness near the River Sora, where he established his own simple, unpretentious Christian community.

Nilus' 'Christian community' stood in stark contrast with the 'Christian civilization' of the day. By the end of the fifteenth century, the church in general, and monasteries in particular, had become very large, powerful institutions. The political power of the feudal state was reinforced by the church hierarchy. As much as one-third of all the available arable land in Russia was controlled by the church, mainly through large monasteries. One monastery — the St. Sergius Monastery of the Trinity — had 100,000 peasants cultivating estates in fifteen provinces. Nilus set up his monastery as the antithesis of this. He and his monks deliberately set aside any quest for power or acquisition of property. They lived as simply as possible, owned no large tracts of land and employed no peasants as labour. They worked humbly with their own hands to support themselves.

For most of the time, Nilus lived his life quietly with his monks at Sora. But from time to time, as a respected scholar, Nilus was asked to attend church synods and speak on the issues under consideration. When he did, Nilus strongly critiqued the church hierarchy's lust for power and the trappings of power. He called on the church to give up its Machiavellian political ambitions, and give away its large monastic landholdings, its jewelled icons and its gold and silver sacramental chalices. Nilus challenged his listeners to remember that 'the primary responsibility of a Christian is to be...as kind as possible.'

> *'This is the primary responsibility of a Christian — to be...as kind as possible in our human relations.'*
> — Nilus Sorsky

Nilus' community was organised to encourage personal liberty in the context of communal responsibility. Nilus didn't set himself up as an authority figure in the monastery, but simply made himself available to the other monks as a fellow traveller on the holy journey. Each monk was encouraged to seek God's will in their own way as part of a company dedicated to following the scriptures. Nilus always pointed to Jesus as the example 'for us all to follow', individually and collectively.

In 1490, Nilus was asked to attend a council convened by the church to decide the fate of a group of heretics known as the 'Judaizers' — a group of people seeking to re-establish the practice of Jewish rites in the Christian church. They were also critical of the growing wealth of the church, and called for the church to repent, empty itself of its pretentiousness and return to a spirituality of simple, dedicated service. Joseph, the abbot of the monastery at Volokolamsk, advocated that the Judaizers be condemned as heretics, arrested and burned alive. He justified his appeal on the grounds that Russia was a Christian state and, in so doing, would be defending Christian civilisation.

Nilus publicly opposed Joseph, arguing that only God was in a position to judge a person's relationship with him, and that no-one else, be they an archbishop or an abbot, had a right to judge. Nilus said that if anyone was concerned for their souls, they should admonish them by their own example. He steadfastly refused to condone the use of corporal punishment, torture and execution by ecclesiastical or civil authorities under any circumstances, advocating clemency and charity as 'more becoming to Christians'.

It was only after Nilus' death in 1508 that Joseph was able to begin his persecution of the Judaizers again — burning their leaders alive and throwing their followers into prison. As a result of his courageous stand, Nilus had been able to restrain the reactionary forces of the church and state for nearly twenty years.

Suggestions for Meditation:
- » What aspect of this story did you relate to most?
- » Which be-attitude do you feel Nilus embodied best?
- » What is the most valuable lesson you can learn from this story?

Remember Jesus said:
'I have set you an example that you should do as I have done for you.'
John 13:15

MENNO SIMONS

The Architect of the Pacifist Faith Communities

Menno Simons was born in 1496 in the small town of Witmarsum in the northern Netherlands. His family were poor peasants — probably dairy farmers. They sent young Menno to school at a local monastery, where he learned Latin and was taught a bit about the church and the church fathers. At the age of 15, Menno entered the novitiate and at 20 became a deacon in the Catholic church.

Menno was appointed as a priest in his father's village of Pingjum. To begin with, he accepted the church traditions he was brought up in. But in 1531, the church-sanctioned execution of Sicke Freeriks Snijder — whom Menno regarded as 'a god-fearing pious hero' — caused Menno to have serious doubts. He started reading the Bible for himself and thinking critically about church traditions in the light of the scriptures.

Menno was not alone in his struggle with the church. The time was rife with ecclesiastical disillusionment and replete with alternative experiments. Menno found himself caught in the middle of the fights between fanatical reformers on the one hand, and reactionary conservatives on the other. And he was critical of both.

Menno was transferred to Witmarsum, where he came into direct contact with 'Ana-baptists' (those who have been 'baptised again'). They attacked tradition, called for conversion, and advocated adult baptism as a sign of being 'truly born again of the spirit'. Menno was attracted to their zeal, but appalled by their intolerance.

While Menno kept his distance, his brother Pieter joined the Anabaptists. This heightened Menno's ambivalence towards the movement. In 1535, when Pieter was among a group of Anabaptists killed for their beliefs, Menno's agony of soul reached fever pitch. What was he going to do? Menno felt he could no longer be a part of a church which had murdered his brother. But he felt loath to join the Anabaptists, because he was revolted by the reign of terror they'd employed to build their 'New Jerusalem' in Münster.

In the summer of 1535, the armies of Bishop von Waldock stormed the city of Münster, destroyed the 'New Jerusalem' community, and killed their leader Jan van Leyden. Persecution swept through Europe like a plague, but Menno felt it was the perfect time for him to publicly throw in his lot with his Anabaptist brethren. Where others could only see risk, Menno saw the opportunity. With their hardcore leaders dead and their militant ideas discredited, Menno realised there was an unprecedented chance to turn the movement into a tough-minded but tender-hearted counter-culture. Obbe Philips — a pacifist Anabaptist leader — ordained Menno as a pastor, and charged him with this task.

For the next three years, Menno travelled continually, visiting members of the 'scattered and dispirited brotherhood'. For Menno, Christ was the cornerstone of the 'true church', out of which he wanted to build his coalition of radical, voluntary, non-violent communities of disciples, committed to mutual help and peace-making. Menno wrote in his Reply to False Accusations: 'We who knew no peace, are called to be a church of peace. The Prince of Peace is Jesus Christ. True Christians do not know vengeance. They are children of peace. Their hearts overflow with peace. Their mouths speak peace, and they walk in the way of peace.' Thus, out of the violence and counter-violence of Münster, the famous Mennist peace church was born.

> *'True Christians do not know vengeance. They walk in the way of peace.'*
> — Menno Simons

Their commitment to peace did not end their persecution. The church treated anyone who would not submit to their authority as heretics, and the state treated anyone who refused to take up arms for them against others as insurrectionists. So the Mennonites were massacred by the allied forces of the church and the state. A price of 500 guilders was placed on his head, so Menno was forced to be constantly on the move to escape pursuit. Anyone who provided him with hospitality risked arrest. Menno said, 'We could not find in all the countries a cabin in which (we) could be put up safely for even half a year.'

On 31 January 1561, Menno Simons died in Schleswig-Holstein. He was survived not only by the family he and his wife Gertrude had raised, but also by the pacifist faith communities they had nurtured. And the Mennist Anabaptists, or Mennonites as they became known, have been a faithful witness to the vital role the church can play — through mutual help and peace-making — for nearly five hundred years.

Suggestions for Meditation:
- » What aspect of this story did you relate to most?
- » Which be-attitude do you feel Menno embodied best?
- » What is the most valuable lesson you can learn from this story?

Remember Jesus said:

'Put your sword away!' *John 18:11*

'All who draw the sword will die by the sword.' *Matthew 26:52*

Endnote

You can contact the Association of Anabaptists in Australia and New Zealand by checking out www.anabaptist.asn.au or by emailing AAANZ@iprimus.com.au

GEORGE FOX

A Witness Against All Violence

George Fox was born in 1624 at Drayton-in-the-Clay, Leicestershire, England. His father was a weaver and a warden in the Church of England. George got little education other than to read and write and study the Bible. At a young age, George was apprenticed as shoemaker, and was given a lot of encouragement by his pious parents to live a life dedicated to the service of God, regardless of his humble status in society.

In 1643, at the age of 19, George had a vision. He'd been in a pub with his mates who had tried to drag him into a drinking match. He'd got disgusted with their stupidity, left the pub and gone home to think about what he really wanted to do with his life. That night George saw a vision in which he believed God told him to 'forsake all', so he left home to travel the length and breadth of the country in search of God's will.

For the next three years, George interviewed clergy all over England in his search for true spirituality. But, George found very little of the 'tender' spirit he was looking for. He became profoundly disillusioned with the priests in mainline churches and turned to the Bible to find the answers to the questions that he sought. As he read the scriptures, George became convinced that the answers could not be found in 'steeple-houses' (what he called 'churches'), but only in the Spirit that brought life to the church at Pentecost.

From then on, using the Bible as his guide, George sought the inspiration of the Spirit directly for himself. Over time, George developed a theology of the 'inner light'; which, he said, the scriptures say 'enlightens every soul that comes into the world'. So for George, the essence of true spirituality was in becoming ever more aware of the inner glow of the Spirit and ever more ready to act according to the Spirit of the gospels.

George felt it was his duty to do what he could 'to save the church from formalism and the world from infidelity'. When he was about 23 years of age, George began preaching. He was a powerful personality and in an argument 'could outshout just about anybody'. It was said: 'He iterated the British Isles, preaching and protesting as no man before him had ever done'. He felt free to interrupt sermons, ask questions, and critique the authorities. He refused to remove his hat in front of an aristocrat, arguing that all people are equal, and therefore no person deserved special treatment because of their position. He advocated that the poor merited just wages for manual labour, challenging maximum wages fixed for farm work. He argued for the people's participation in both church and state, and equal rights for women as well as men. Needless to say, George offended just about everybody who was somebody in the society of his day. People got so mad at him that they would shake with rage. He would pray for them, and they would often quake with apprehension and trepidation. And that's how George and his supporters became known as the 'Quakers'. Not because of their nervousness, but because of the cultural earthquake they caused wherever they went.

The Sermon On The Mount was the Quaker manifesto. In accordance with their manifesto, the Quakers — or the 'Friends', as they preferred to be called — refused to take oaths, any oaths, including any oaths of loyalty to the government. Because they were already considered troublemakers, their refusal to swear loyalty to the government was taken as a threat to national security. In the three years from 1655 to 1658, when Oliver Cromwell was Lord Protector of the Commonwealth, over 3,000 Quakers were imprisoned. And in the twenty-five years from 1660 to 1685, when Charles II was King of England, over 13,000 Quakers were imprisoned. Through those times, when the Friends were being unjustly incarcerated, tortured and killed in prison, they stayed true to the practice of non-violence that they believed Christ advocated in the Sermon on the Mount. George wrote to 'all friends everywhere' saying 'this I charge you, which is the word of the Lord God unto you all — live in peace, in Christ, the way of peace, and seek the peace of all men and no man's hurt (sic)'.

In 1652, George met Margaret Fell, who became a good Friend. After her husband's death in 1658, George married Margaret. And Margaret became the key organizer of the Society of Friends that they established. Though married, George was seldom at home. Most of the time, George was either on the road or in prison. George not only travelled round the British Isles, but also ventured across Europe and America. When he was in America, George stayed with Native Americans and spoke out against the slavery of Afro-Americans. Leonard Ravenhill says that given George's commitment to justice, it's not surprising that 'no other religious reformer was imprisoned as many times.' While in custody, George used to share the gospel with his prison warders. He would beg them to break their swords, and join him in his liberating campaign for non-violence. George wrote: 'I was never in a prison that it was not the means of bringing multitudes out of their prisons.'

Gorge Fox died in London in 1691. According to the famous historian, Thomas Carlyle, 'the most remarkable incident in modern history is not (Napoleon Bonaparte's) battle of Austerlitz, but George Fox's battle for (the truth) against intolerance'.

Suggestions for Meditation:
» What aspect of this story did you relate to most?
» Which be-attitude do you feel George embodied best?
» What is the most valuable lesson you can learn from this story?

Remember Jesus said:
'Do not react to an evil person.
If someone strikes you on the right cheek, turn the other also.'
Matthew 5:39

NIKOLAUS LUDWIG

The Count Who Cared

Nikolaus Ludwig, Count von Zinzendorf, was born in Dresden in 1700.

His father, a cabinet minister in Saxony, died when Nikolaus was only six weeks old, and he was brought up by his grandmother who was a Pietist. The Pietist movement emphasized a religion of the 'heart.' So Nikolaus grew up with a passionate spirituality.

At the age of ten Nikolaus was sent to grammar school. There Nikolaus met up with five other boys who were as devout as he was. Together they founded 'The Order Of The Grain Of Mustard Seed', pledging themselves to 'love the whole human family'.

Nikolaus went on to study law at Wittenberg and, after graduating, joined the civil service. Before settling down, he travelled round Europe. In an art gallery in Dusseldorf, Nikolaus found himself face to face with a painting by Feti of Jesus before Pilate, wearing a crown of thorns. The inscription read: 'All this I did for you. What are you doing for me?' In answer to the question, Nikolaus decided he needed to leave the civil service, and find the work Christ wanted him to do.

In 1722, Nikolaus was approached by some Moravian refugees with a request to settle on his lands. He granted their request, and a small band crossed them to settle in a town they called Herrnhut, or 'the Lord's Watch.' Nikolaus was intrigued by the story of these Moravian 'Unitas Fratrum', and studied the history of the devout 'United Brethren'.

As it turned out, the 'United Brethren' were not very 'united' at the time. In fact, they were going through a period of serious communal discord. So in 1727, Nikolaus decided to work full-time with the troubled Moravian community. Eventually, Nikolaus was able to help resolve the conflicts, and broker the 'Brotherly Agreement' — a document that set out the guidelines for Christian conduct — that became the framework for life at Herrnhut.

Following the resolution of the conflict, the community experienced a period of incredible renewal, described by some observers as the 'Moravian Pentecost'. As a result of this renascence there was an increased interest in love feasts, songfests, prayer and mission. They established a twenty-four-hour-a-day prayer watch that continued for the next hundred years. And they developed a mission movement that encircled the world.

In 1731, while attending the coronation of Christian VI in Copenhagen, Nikolaus met Anthony Ulrich, a converted slave from the West Indies. Nikolaus brought Anthony back with him to Herrnhut, and encouraged him to tell everybody his story. The tale of his people's plight so moved the Moravians, that two young men, Leonard Dober and David Nitchmann, were sent to live among the slaves and share the gospel.

> *'I have one passion. It is Christ, and Christ alone!'*
> — Nikolaus Ludwig

In 1732, the Moravians sent their first mission to the slaves on St. Thomas in the Virgin Islands. And, in 1733, they sent their second mission to Greenland. Then, in 1734, they sent their third mission to St. Croix, also in the Virgin Islands. Ten people in the third mission died in the first year; but others volunteered to take their place.

The Moravians sent missions to Surinam (1735), South Africa (1737), the North American Indians (1740), Jamaica (1754), and Antigua (1756). Between 1732 and 1760, 226 Moravians went to ten different far-flung countries, doing more mission work in thirty years than Anglicans and Protestants had done during the two preceding centuries.

Meanwhile, John and Charles Wesley were converted through their association with Moravians, and went on to found the Methodist Church which also made another amazing contribution to holistic global mission.

In 1737, Nikolaus was elected as bishop to guide the movement. He travelled widely to encourage the movement's missions, which expanded rapidly to embrace America, Russia, Africa, and Asia. Wherever he went, Nikolaus encouraged Christian groups to cooperate with one another. And, history seems to suggest that it was Nikolaus who first advocated evangelical 'ecumenism' as we know it today.

In 1760, Nikolaus died at the age of sixty, having done his best for fifty years to be true to the pledge he made at the age of ten — to 'love the whole human family'!

Suggestions for Meditation:
» What aspect of this story did you relate to most?
» Which be-attitude do you feel Nikolaus embodied best?
» What is the most valuable lesson you can learn from this story?

Remember Jesus said:
'Love one another.
As I have loved you, so must you love one another.' *John 13:34*

JOHN WESLEY

The Whole World Is My Parish

John Wesley was born in 1703 into a robust extended Christian family environment, animated by rigorous devotion and vigorous debate. His home was a Church Rectory in Lincolnshire, England.

His grandparents consistently advocated a nonconformist view of faith. And, though his father was a bit of a traditionalist, it was his mother — who promoted the evangelical cause with a passion — who did most to shape the young John Wesley.

After school, John and his younger brother Charles went to Oxford University together where they started, of all things, a group called 'The Holy Club'.

In 1737, the Wesley brothers travelled to America on behalf of the Society for the Propagation of the Gospel. On the way the Wesleys met some Moravian Christians. And, by all accounts, it was a meeting made in heaven. For it was through the Moravians that John was introduced to a deeper, more personal, more profound experience of the Grace of God than he had ever had before. His heart was 'strangely warmed', and his ministry was 'totally transformed' forever.

Over the next fifty years John rode over two hundred and fifty thousand miles on horseback, travelling the length and breadth of Britain, to preach his gospel of amazing grace to rich and poor alike. At daybreak you would often find John preaching in the fields to the laborers on their way to work, while at midday you would find him making his way to the village square, to preach to the crowds thronging round the merchants in the market place. And at the end of the day you would often find John meeting with people who had responded to his preaching, and who wanted him to preach some more.

All in all he is said to have preached some fifty thousand sermons. John's message was the simple proclamation of the love of God revealed to us in Jesus. John pleaded with people to open their hearts to the Spirit of Jesus, so that he could fill their lives with his love to overflowing. John expected that as people's lives were filled with the Spirit, they would spontaneously get involved with causes that were close to the Spirit's heart.

John particularly hoped people would join him in sharing the good news of God's love with the destitute, who felt that God had abandoned them. 'I have only one point of view,' he said, 'to promote as far as I am able, vital practical religion, and (so) preserve the life of God in the soul of humanity.'

In 1742, John set up 'class meetings' for his converts, to equip them to carry out their great commission. Each meeting had a leader and a dozen members. In each meeting each member was expected to give an account of the progress they were making in seeking to make the two great commandments — to love God and to love their neighbour — a reality in their lives.

> *'I have only one point of view: to promote, as far as I am able, vital practical religion, and (so) preserve the life of God in the soul of humanity.'*
> — John Wesley

It was a stroke of genius, the 'method' of the 'methodists', and it unleashed what was referred to as 'the unspeakable usefulness' of a mass movement made up of a large dynamic network of small discipleship groups.

Consequently, by the end of the 1700s these 'methodists' were the most disciplined, cohesive, and self-conscious body of people in England.

They campaigned against the slave trade, opened up clinics, dispensed medicines and gave services freely to those in need, set up revolving loan funds for the poor, worked to solve the problem of unemployment, and agitated for prison, liquor, and labor reform.

John was rejected by the powerful figures of both church and state whom he denounced as a 'generation of triflers', but common people embraced him as one of their own.

He died in London on 2 March 1791.

Suggestions for Meditation:
» What aspect of this story did you relate to most?
» Which be-attitude do you feel John embodied best?
» What is the most valuable lesson you can learn from this story?

Remember Jesus said:
'The Spirit of the Lord is on me,
  because he has anointed me to preach good news to the poor.'
Luke 4:18

CHARLES FINNEY

Christ's Lawyer

Charles Finney was born in 1792 in Connecticut, and raised on a farm in Oneida, New York State. He was a big, strong, healthy boy who couldn't remember being sick a day in his life.

Charles enjoyed working hard on the farm, and then taking time out to play in the forest and sail on the lakes. He loved music, learning to compose, and to sing and play the violin and the cello with a passion. He also loved study, reading everything he could lay his hands on — from histories and biographies to philosophies.

Charles grew into a formidable, intelligent, and multi-talented young man who was only saved from taking himself too seriously by an irrepressible sense of humour. From the age of sixteen to twenty, he taught in a progressive, experimental, student-centred school at Henderson. He joined in games before and after class, so it's not surprising that his students loved him.

In 1812, war was declared against Britain, and Charles was one of the first to enlist to fight for his country. But he became disillusioned with the indiscipline of the troops, the incompetence of their commanders, and the questionable nature of their cause. So he packed his bags and came home.

In 1814, Charles went to New Jersey, where he taught school during the day and learned Latin, Greek and Maths at night. He excelled in his self-guided studies, but never got a college degree. In 1818, Charles went to Adams, where he read law and became a law clerk. In 1820, he was admitted to the profession, and began to practise as a lawyer.

Charles had always attended church, but more for the music than the message. He loved anthems, but hated sermons. He despised 'the lack of reason in religion', and would regularly take a minister aside on a Monday to shred the homily he had delivered on a Sunday.

Through this, Charles began to study the Bible for himself. As a result of his study, on 10 October 1821, Charles was miraculously converted. The very next day he publicly announced, in his own inimitable style, 'I have taken a retainer from the Lord Jesus Christ to plead his cause!' And 'plead his cause' he did.

To begin with, people thought the conversion story was a practical joke. But as time went by, they realised Charles was very serious indeed.

He called his choir together, confessed he'd been an unbeliever, and begged them to join him on his journey towards faith. He delivered a series of lectures to the Bench and Bar of Rochester, New York, not to reject religion, but to accept it, and to be committed as lawyers to the Law of God. It wasn't long before he was preaching to large crowds all over New York State.

> *'Revivals are hindered when churches take wrong ground in regard to any question involving human rights.'*
> — *Charles Finney, Lectures on Revivals of Religion*

Charles' preaching was a potent mixture of sustained intellectual argument and impassioned emotional appeal, delivered in a strong, imaginative, colloquial, popular style. As Christ's lawyer, he pleaded for people to be converted, 'repent from selfishness', and participate in 'the reforms of the age'.

Charles was particularly appalled at his country's war against Mexico. He said: 'There can scarcely be conceived a more abominable maxim than "Our country right or wrong"', challenging the church not to support the prosecution of what he saw as an imperialist war. He denounced the war as a 'selfish war', declaring that, as such, it was 'wholesale murder' and 'for a person to aid or abet the prosecution of (this) war involves the guilt of murder.'

Furthermore, he said, it was 'horrible' to even 'think of fighting in defence of a nation, proclaiming the inalienable right to liberty' while 'standing with its proud foot on the neck of three million crushed and prostrate slaves'. He begged the church to work for repentance and restitution, emancipation and reparation.

So, in 1835, when Charles went to help set up the theology program at Oberlin College, he made sure that it was not only co-educational and inclusive of 'coloured' students, but also committed to the anti-slavery campaign. Both staff and students at Oberlin publicly opposed the Fugitive Slave Bill, administered a fund to help runaway slaves, and developed one of the most important stations on the Underground Railroad for escaped slaves. On one famous occasion in 1858, hundreds of people from the college marched into town and stormed a hotel where an escaped slave was being held captive. They brought him back to Oberlin, where he stayed in the home of the Professor of Moral Philosophy, before he was spirited off on the road to freedom.

Charles Finney died in 1875. It is said that up to a million people were converted through his ministry.

Suggestions for Meditation:
- What aspect of this story did you relate to most?
- Which be-attitude do you feel Charles embodied best?
- What is the most valuable lesson you can learn from this story?

Remember Jesus said:

'Seek first the kingdom of God and his righteousness.'

Matthew 6:33

SOJOURNER TRUTH

'Ain't I A Woman?'

Sojourner Truth was born in 1797, one of thirteen children born to slave parents in a little Dutch settlement in New York State in the United States of America. She was given a Dutch name – Isabella Baumfree – and brought up speaking Dutch. It was only when she was sold to an English-speaking master that she learnt to speak English, with a strong Dutch accent.

Isabella never got to know her brothers and sisters, because they were sold off one by one as slaves. Isabella herself was first sold at the tender age of eleven. By the time she was sold, the young Isabella was able to take with her a strong faith and an indefatigable dignity that her mother had managed to cultivate in her daughter's heart.

Isabella was bought and sold twice. Her third master, John Dumont, stood out as a 'cruel man', even in those times, when casual cruelty was so common it usually went unnoticed. Dumont forced the young Isabella to marry an older slave named Thomas, with whom she had five children. And, one by one, Dumont sold off Isabella's children as slaves.

As a result of the pressure exerted by the growing anti-slavery movement, Dumont promised Isabella her freedom. However, he reneged on his promise. So, in 1827, Isabella ran away with the last of her children. A few months later, in 1828, slavery was finally abolished in New York State. Isabella and her infant son were free at last.

Isabella moved to New York City, where she worked as a domestic servant in a few different religious communities. For a while she stayed with a Quaker family. They helped her get back one of her children, and gave her a basic education.

While slavery had been abolished in New York State, it was still in force in other states. So, once she got on her feet, Isabella decided to take up the cause of her enslaved sisters. In 1843, she changed her name to Sojourner Truth, and she hit the hustings, speaking out on behalf of her sisters still in bondage, rallying support for abolition.

In Northhampton, Massachusetts, Sojourner came across a radical community that went by the pedestrian name of 'The Northhampton Association For Education and Industry'. In the community Sojourner met fellow abolitionists, who supported her ministry, and helped her tell her story. In 1850, *The Narrative Of Sojourner Truth* was published.

Sojourner spent months on the road at a time preaching 'God's truth and plan for salvation', working tirelessly to free her fellow slaves, and lobbying the government to give freed slaves land of their own. And so Sojourner became the national symbol of the struggle.

Sojourner was a tall woman, powerfully built, with a big booming voice, and a spellbinding preacher. One moment she would throw the book at her audience, and the next moment she would lead them in song to repentance. It was said that 'no one who met her could forget her.'

Perhaps the most famous message Sojourner preached was 'Ain't I A Woman?', which she delivered at the Women's Rights Convention in Akron, Ohio in 1851, and which has since come to be regarded as one of the great speeches on women's rights of all time (see below).

Sojourner continued to preach on human rights until her ill health forced her to retire to her home in Battle Creek, Michigan, where she died in 1883.

'Ain't I A Woman?'

> That man over there says that women need
> to be helped into carriages, and lifted over ditches,
> and to have the best place everywhere.
> Nobody helps me any best place.
> And ain't I a woman?
> Look at me! Look at my arm!
> I have ploughed, I have planted
> and I have gathered into barns.
> And no man could head me.
> And ain't I a woman?
> I could work as much, and eat as much as a man —
> when I could get it —
> and bear the lash as well!
> And ain't I a woman?
> I have borne children and seen most of them sold into slavery,
> and when I cried out with a mother's grief, none but Jesus
> heard me.
> And ain't I a woman?
> That little man in black there!

He says women can't have as much rights as men,
'cause Christ wasn't a woman.
Where did your Christ come from?
From God and a Woman! Man had nothing to do with him!
If the first woman God ever made was strong enough
to turn the world upside down all alone,
these women together ought to be able to turn it back
and get it right-side up again.
And now that they are asking to do it, the men better let them.

Suggestions for Meditation:
» What aspect of this story did you relate to most?
» Which be-attitude do you feel Sojourner embodied best?
» What is the most valuable lesson you can learn from this story?

Remember Jesus said:
'He has sent me to proclaim
freedom for the prisoners, release to the oppressed.' *Luke 4:18*

CAROLINE CHISHOLM

A Woman's Woman

Caroline was born into a wealthy rural English family in 1808.

The Jones were evangelical Christians. Her father brought his daughter up to stand by what she believed in, and her mother brought her daughter up to serve the poor.

So the fun-loving young Caroline grew up with a serious faith, a strong mind, and a social conscience.

Caroline's father died when she was young, and her erstwhile wealthy family was suddenly plunged into desperate poverty. It was one thing for her to care for the poor; it was another thing for her to *be* poor herself. It was an experience Caroline never forgot.

When she reached a marriageable age, Caroline met Archibald Chisholm. He was an English Officer in the Indian Army. He cut a dashing figure in his uniform; and when she got the chance to talk with him, Caroline found Archy had substance as well as style. So they decided to get married.

The Chisholms' was anything but a traditional marriage. They decided their marriage would be 'an equal partnership', as opposed to the 'superior-subordinate relationships' which were more common at the time. And though Caroline, who was Protestant, agreed to become Catholic like Archie, she only agreed on the proviso that she would be free to pursue any non-denominational philanthropic work that she felt called to — 'without impediment'.

After their wedding Archie was recalled to India, and Caroline was to follow him later to Madras. Upon her arrival the officers' wives drew her into their party circuit — but Caroline loathed the petty gossip that filled the empty lives of the *burri memsahibs*.

Caroline's eye was caught more by the poverty than by the opulence. And she immediately began to pray that God would show her a way to respond to the plight of the hapless child prostitutes that swarmed around the outskirts of the garrison town.

Caroline eventually decided that the only way she could save the poor kids from prostitution — or marriages, so degrading that they were almost as bad — was to start a school, which could teach them marketable skills.

The officers — and their wives — were scandalized by Caroline's 'unbecoming' behaviour, and told Archie to pull his wife into line, or risk becoming a 'social outcast'.

But Archie refused to be bullied; throwing his lot in with the 'social outcasts', by personally underwriting the expenses of the school himself.

> *'I am not one of those who like to ask 'What will the Government do for us?' The question of the day is, 'What shall we do for ourselves?''*
> — Caroline

So, with Archie's support, Caroline set up a modern school in Madras — teaching not only reading and writing, but also cooking and cleaning, budgeting and bookkeeping, and even nursing, to street kids.

Some years later, due to ill health, Archie and Caroline applied to take long leave in Australia. So they arrived in Sydney with their two children in 1838, and settled into a comfortable house in Windsor.

After a couple of years Archie had to go back to his regiment, but they decided it was best for Caroline and the children to stay on at their new home in New South Wales.

Caroline thought she might open a school in Sydney like she had in Madras. But as she prayed about it, Caroline became convinced she needed to set the idea of a school aside for a while, and get involved with the poor immigrant women — penniless widows and orphaned girls who slept in tents in the Domain or in the streets around The Rocks.

Many of the women that Caroline met told tragic tales of fleeing destitution in England by emigrating to Australia; only to fall into the hands of abusive crews on board the ships, and unscrupulous brothel owners once the ships docked in Sydney harbour.

Upon hearing these stories, Caroline made it her business to meet every ship as it came in. To start with, Caroline took these women into her own home at Windsor. Then, when there were too many, she persuaded the wife of Governor Gipps to get her husband to make the old barracks on Bent Street available to her. And she turned the rat-infested shed into an emergency shelter, accommodating more than a hundred women at one time.

Caroline then accompanied the residents around town in their search for work. When she couldn't find enough jobs around Sydney, she set up voluntary committees all around New South Wales to act as employment agencies for her. And she personally took her charges from Moreton Bay to Port Macquarie to secure proper employment for them.

In the process, Caroline secured employment for over fourteen thousand women. And to protect the rights of these women, Caroline introduced employment contracts, in triplicate, to ensure the provision of good basic conditions in their place of employment.

When Archie returned in 1845, Caroline talked to him about the need to take her campaign to Britain, in order to lobby the British Government directly. So Archie agreed to return with Caroline to England to take the fight for the rights of migrants to their point of origin.

Back in England Caroline met with the Secretary of State, the Home Secretary, and the Land and Emigration Commissioners, providing them with detailed reports on human rights abuses, and presenting them with specific policy options which they could adopt to address these issues.

While waiting for these reforms to be adopted, Caroline went ahead and organised a society to aid migrants, independent of, but in cooperation with, the British Government. The central committee of the society she organised, under the high-profile presidency of Lord Ashley MP (Earl of Shaftesbury), with the public support of Charles Dickens, set up a scheme to help poor migrants with everything from safe travel to personal loans.

Caroline did all she could to expedite family reunions for ex-convicts, who were separated from their wives and children for years. She lobbied for free passage for these reunions, and for land reform to enable these families to get small farms of their own.

In 1854, Caroline joined Archie in Melbourne where, since 1851, he had been running the Aussie end of their operation. Back in Australia Caroline continued her relentless campaign through the press and the parliament for women's entitlements.

By 1866 the Chisholms had exhausted their considerable intellectual, emotional and physical resources. They had worked passionately, without pay, in the service of humanity, for more than a quarter of a century. And when they retired to England they were worn out. In 1877 Caroline died, and her beloved Archie died a few months later.

Suggestions for Meditation:
» What aspect of this story did you relate to most?
» Which be-attitude do you feel Caroline embodied best?
» What is the most valuable lesson you can learn from this story?

Remember Jesus said:
'Love your neighbor as yourself.' *Matthew 22:39*

TE WHITI

The Forgotten Forerunner of Non-violent Resistance

Te Whiti* was born in Parihaka, Aotearoa (New Zealand) about 1815. His Maori parents, Hone Kakahi and Raumahora, made sure Te Whiti was brought up well-schooled in the values of traditional Maori culture. A Maori preacher, Minarapa Te Rangihatuake, taught the young Te Whiti to read and write and study the scriptures, and a Lutheran missionary, Johannes Riemenschneider, baptised him. Throughout his life, Te Whiti constantly struggled to relate a personal Christian faith to traditional Maori culture.

On 30 April 1864, many Maori warriors died in the Battle of Sentry Hill, trying to defend their land from further European incursions. Te Whiti didn't take up arms, but supported his people's defence of their land. The New Zealand Settlements Act authorised the confiscation of any land where the government deemed the natives to be in rebellion. Although the judiciary warned that confiscation was illegal, the government systematically took over 4 million hectares of land. Much of that was in Taranaki.

In the 1870s, more immigrants arrived from Europe. The government was pressured to provide more land for the Pakeha (white people). As a result, surveyors began slicing up the Waimate Plains. To start with, Te Whiti and his people allowed this to happen, but in the late 1870s, when the settlers began to move in, the people of Parihaka chose to act.

Te Whiti said: 'My name is taken from the hill Puke Te Whiti (which stands as a sentinel guarding the past, the present and the future). Like Puke Te Whiti, I stand as a sentinel — not one bit of land will be given over to strangers with my consent.'

Te Whiti chose to fight, but unlike his forbears, he chose to fight the invasion non-violently. Publicly, he declared, 'Let not the Pakehas think to succeed by reason of their guns...I want not war, but they do. The flashes of their guns have singed our eyelashes, and yet they say they do not want war...Though some, in darkness of heart, seeing their land ravished, might wish to take arms and kill the aggressors, I say it must not be!'

'Stout-hearted patience' became the spiritual dynamic of Te Whiti's campaign of non-violent resistance. Te Whiti said to his people: 'This is my word to you to the tribe...There are two roads, one to life and one to death. God said, in the days of Noah, the earth will be destroyed; build an ark, or all will perish. Noah did as he was commanded and this was an example for us to follow. God said to Lot, depart from the city; leave your houses and goods, for he who turns back shall die, and the city shall be burnt. God said to Moses, do not strive against me, or you will die; by faith only can this tribe be saved. This is an example to us. Our salvation today is stout-heartedness and patience.'

Having found the dynamic he needed, Te Whiti searched the scriptures for a tactic he could use for his campaign. He came across a verse in Isaiah 2:4 that spoke about 'beating swords into plough-shares'. As soon as he read it, Te Whiti knew he had the tactic he needed to devise a strategy of effective resistance. Te Whiti exhorted his warriors to fight against the Europeans who were invading their land without weapons — by simply taking their ploughs and ploughing their own lands — patiently, persistently, and relentlessly ploughing over any and all of the crops that had been planted by the Europeans on the lands they had stolen.

> *'Go, put your hands to the plough. Look not back. If any come with guns and swords, be not afraid. If they smite you, smite not in return. If they rend you, be not discouraged. Another will take up the good work.'*
> *— Te Whiti*

Te Whiti said to his ploughmen: 'Go, put your hands to the plough. Look not back. If any come with guns and swords, be not afraid. If they smite you, smite not in return. If they rend you, be not discouraged. Another will take up the good work. If evil thoughts fill the minds of the settlers, and they flee from their farms to the town as in the war of old, enter not you into their houses, touch not their goods nor their cattle. My eye is over all.'

During the campaign, hundreds of Te Whiti's ploughmen were arrested and imprisoned without trial. But still the ploughmen kept on ploughing — demanding the government recognize their ownership of the land.

On 5 November 1881, 1500 volunteers and members of the Armed Constabulary invaded Parihaka. Some 2000 of the people from Parihaka allowed themselves to be arrested by the troops without retaliation. Te Whiti was one of the first to be led away to imprisonment without trial. However, he continued to demand that his people be treated justly, and that the Europeans return their tribal lands to them. After he returned to Taranaki in 1883, Te Whiti continued his campaign of non-violent resistance in one way or another until the day that he died in 1907.

Parihaka historian, Te Miringa, claims Te Whiti was the forerunner of the modern movement for nonviolent resistance. He says Mahatma Gandhi learnt about Te Whiti from an Irish delegation that visited Parihaka. The rest is history.

*Te Whiti: 'wh' in Maori is pronounced as 'ph' in English — so Te Whiti is pronounced 'Te Phiti.'

Suggestions for Meditation:

» What aspect of this story did you relate to most?
» Which be-attitude do you feel Te Whiti embodied best?
» What is the most valuable lesson you can learn from this story?

Remember Jesus said:

'Love your enemies –
and pray for those who persecute you.'
Matthew 5:44

FLORENCE NIGHTINGALE

The Lady of the Lamp

Florence Nightingale was born in 1820, the daughter of wealthy English parents, William and Fanny Nightingale, who had inherited a large fortune. Florence, and her sister Parthenope, were tutored in languages, history, and mathematics by their father, and in etiquette, society, and manners by their mother.

When Florence was twelve years old she was riding a pony near her family estate in Hampshire, when she came across a shepherd whose dog had broken its leg. The shepherd told Florence that the dog was going to have to be put down. But Florence would not hear of it. She immediately took charge of the situation, binding the broken leg and tending the dog's wounds until the animal recovered.

At the age of seventeen Florence wrote in her diary, 'God spoke to me and called me to His service.' When Florence told her parents that she felt called to serve God by becoming a nurse, and caring for the sick, William and Fanny were mortified. In those days hospitals were squalid establishments, and the nurses who worked in them were as disreputable as the institutions they served. Willam and Fanny had 'far nobler things' in mind for Florence than becoming a 'mere nurse'! But Florence would not be dissuaded from pursuing her call to nursing.

In 1845, she began visiting hospitals to study how they operated for herself. In 1851, she persuaded her parents to permit her to train as a nurse at the Institute of Protestant Deaconnesses in Kaiserwerth, in Germany. And, in 1853, upon her return to England, she accepted a position as Superintendent of the Institution for the Care of Sick Gentlewomen in London.

Florence seized the opportunity that appointment provided to turn the Institution for the Care of Sick Gentlewomen into a model hospital of the times — putting bells in wards so that patients could call nurses when they needed them, and training the nurses to give quality care when called upon to do so.

Meanwhile, war broke out in the Crimea. News filtered back from the front that the wounded were being treated appallingly, often being left to die of dysentry on make-shift beds of filthy straw. The Secretary Of War, Sydney Herbert, asked Florence if she would do something about the situation. Two days later Florence found herself on the way to the major hospital in Scutari, Turkey, with thirty-four of her nurses. Florence was determined to do her utmost to provide the best care that she could, but when she arrived she found herself blocked at every turn. On the one hand were the misogynist military bureaucrats who didn't want to lift a finger to help the 'interfering women'. On the other hand there were the doctors, who didn't want to be upstaged by nurses in their own hospital. But Florence was undaunted by these obstructions and confronted them fearlessly.

> *'I have simply done my Master's work.'*
> — Florence

'The very essence of Truth seemed to emanate from her,' wrote an awestruck William Richmond. She had, he said, 'a perfect fearlessness in telling it!'

Florence broke army regulations that got in the way of getting what she needed for the men in her care. To anyone who had the temerity to try to tell her that something 'could not be done', she countered, quickly, 'but it plain must be done!'

However, Florence never demanded any more from others than she demanded of herself. She was on call twenty-four hours a day. She accompanied her patients into the operating theatre, and, as chloroform had not yet been invented, stayed with them through the operation to soothe their pain. She often spent eight hours a day on her wards, cleaning, tending and binding the wounds of the wounded. Then, before she retired, she would light a lamp, and walk through the wards — walk by the four miles of men, in beds lined up side by side, in the military hospital — just to make sure they were as comfortable as they could be for the night. Legend has it, that the men used to kiss her shadow as she passed by.

Though emaciated and exhausted, Florence refused to leave Scutari until all the soldiers were evacuated in July 1856. When she returned home, the 'Lady of the Lamp' was a hero. But Florence spurned the spot light. She didn't make any public appearances or give any interviews to the press. Instead, for the next sixteen years she invested her time in training nurses and working tirelessly for real health reform.

Over time her own health began to fail, and by 1896, Florence herself became completely bedridden. For her heroic efforts in transforming the nursing profession, in 1907 the bedridden Florence Nightingale became the first woman to be awarded the British Order Of Merit. Florence was quoted as saying, 'I have simply done my Master's work.' And, having done so, in 1910 she died.

Suggestions for Meditation:
- What aspect of this story did you relate to most?
- Which be-attitude do you feel Florence embodied best?
- What is the most valuable lesson you can learn from this story?

Remember Jesus said:

'The more important matters of the law (are) —
justice, mercy and fidelity.' *Matthew 23:23*

HENRI DUNANT

Founder of the Red Cross

Henri Dunant was born in Geneva, Switzerland on 8 May 1828. He was brought up in a devout Reformed Church family who were involved in an evangelical awakening that was committed to fidelity and generosity. Young Henri didn't do well in his studies, but he did win the school piety prize. When he grew older, Henri joined the *Societé Evangelique*, flourishing spiritually under the guidance of Pastor Louis Gaussen.

In 1848, at the age of twenty, Henri organised the Union of Geneva to 'heat up lukewarm believers', to fire them up and to make them 'more effective in Christian charity'. The Young Men's Christian Association (YMCA) had been started in London a few years earlier; and Henri linked the Geneva Union with it, encouraging the YMCA to become an international movement in 1855.

Meanwhile, Henri was developing his business. He travelled to Algeria, where he wanted to set up a wheat mill, but couldn't get the necessary approval. Henri decided to approach the Emperor and ask him for permission directly. Napoleon III was leading the French army against the Austrian army who had invaded neighbouring Italy. Henri arrived at Solferino to meet the Emperor a day after a French victory had left 40,000 dead. Wounded men lay on the battlefield. Henri instantly set aside his business and any plans he had to speak to the Emperor, and turned his attention to the casualities in desperate need of help.

In those days, a severe wound was a death sentence. Most armies not only had no effective way of caring for the wounded, but saw doctors and nurses from the other side as combatants, and would fire at them. So the wounded were often left to die where they fell. But, despite the risks, Henri could not leave them there. He organised a group of nearby townspeople to help. He got the wounded moved into homes and churches, even a local castle. And he got his volunteers to treat the wounded — friend or foe — as brothers. He went about his work crying 'Tutti fratelli! Tutti fratelli!' — 'All are brothers! All are brothers!'

Solferino changed Henri's life forever. Henri was appalled at the carnage of war, and committed himself to do whatever he could to reduce the suffering associated with it. He wrote a book entitled

A Memory of Solferino. It included eyewitness accounts of the battle and its brutal aftermath, and it contained an idea about forming an international society of volunteers committed to caring for the victims of war. *A Memory of Solferino* was published in 1862, and it stirred influential people all over Europe to act and to act quickly.

> *'I am a disciple of Christ — simply that.'*
> — Henri Dunant

On 9 February 1863, Gustav Moynier put Henri's proposals before the Geneva Society for Public Welfare. The society decided to set up a permanent international committee, including Moynier and two well-known physicians, with Switzerland's leading soldier as chairman and Henri as secretary, to implement Henri's plans. On 26 October 1863, 36 delegates from 14 countries met in Geneva to organise the work of what was to become known as the Red Cross, and lobby for international recognition of what was to become known as the Geneva Convention. On 8 August 1864, 24 official delegates from 16 European governments met to formally agree to the terms of the first Geneva Convention. It was also agreed that the symbol of the movement would be a red cross on a white background, the opposite of the Swiss flag. And Dr Appia, one of the founding physicians, first wore the red cross on his sleeve in the Prussian-Danish war later that year.

While Henri was becoming the architect of a global benevolent organisation, his Swiss business was falling apart. He had spent a lot of his time, money and energy on his humanitarian work, at the expense of his financial ventures and, in 1867, he was declared bankrupt. A story by his colleagues, blaming him for the collapse of their enterprise, was published in the newspaper. He promised to pay his creditors, but it was a great scandal, and Henri was forced to resign from the Red Cross.

Henri fled Geneva and made his way to Paris. But he didn't find any work, and was reduced to sleeping on park benches. For the next twenty-five years, he wandered round Europe, destitute. Then, in 1892, he returned to Switzerland and was given shelter in a hospital in the village of Heiden, where he was to stay for the rest of his life.

In 1895, a young journalist heard there was a man staying in the hospital who claimed to have started the Red Cross. So he went to investigate. He found Henri, interviewed him, and printed his amazing story. Once his story was known, Henri was fêted by society. In 1901, Henri was given the Nobel Peace Prize. But he spent none of the prize money on himself; instead he made bequests to people who had helped him, and funded a free room in the hospital for the poor of Heiden who needed medical treatment.

Henri Dunant died in Heiden on 30 October 1910. The anniversary of his birth is now World Red Cross Day.

The Geneva Convention agreed on the obligation of armies to collect the wounded; for their captors to treat wounded enemy soldiers; for all ambulances, hospitals, and medical workers and their equipment to be recognized as neutrals; for all local inhabitants treating the wounded to be recognized as neutrals; and for the red cross to be honored as a symbol of protection and neutral assistance in times of war.

Suggestions for Meditation:
» What aspect of this story did you relate to most?
» Which be-attitude do you feel Henri embodied best?
» What is the most valuable lesson you can learn from this story?

Remember Jesus said:
'You are all brothers (and sisters)!' *Matthew 23:8*

JOSEPH DE VEUSTER

Damien the Leper

On 3 January 1840, a boy was born into a family of farmers at Tremeloo, Belgium. They called their son 'Joseph' — Joseph De Veuster. His mother was very religious, and she encouraged her son to go to the College of Braine-le-Comte and join the Fathers of the Sacred Heart. In 1860, when 'Joseph' entered the order, he took the name 'Damien'.

In 1864, Damien volunteered to go as a missionary to Hawaii. He was ordained in Honolulu, and spent the next nine years evangelising the people of Puno and Kohala. During that time, nearly eight hundred people were diagnosed as lepers, rounded up under the orders of the Board of Health — which the locals called the 'Board of Death' — and banished to the island of Molokai, where they were left to die. Damien wrote: 'Many Christians at Kohala also had to go to Molokai. Eight years among Christians you love, and who love you, have tied powerful bonds. I can only attribute to God an undeniable feeling that soon I shall join them.'

In May 1873, Damien was granted his request to go to Molokai. However, the Church sent him with little more than their blessing. He took no resources — apart from his breviary — to start his mission in the Kalawao Leper Colony. When Damien arrived, he found a dilapidated church in a demoralised community. There was no place for him to stay, so he camped under a pandanus tree near the church. A large rock beside the tree served as his desk and dining table.

Damien couldn't help but hear the wracking coughs of the chronically ill people all around him during the night. At daybreak he set out to visit them, and it was as if he'd opened a door to a parallel universe and stepped into a world 'scarcely less dreadful than hell itself'. He came face to face with men and women whose bodies were ravaged by the voracious bacillus of leprosy. In one of his first visits, he came across a young girl in a terrible state. The whole side of her body had been eaten away by worms. He found the stench of rotting flesh the hardest part to cope with. 'Many a time,' he wrote, 'I have been obliged to remain outside to breathe fresh air. To counteract the bad smell I use tobacco. The smell of the pipe preserved me from the odour of our lepers.'

Damien was determined to do all he could to demonstrate God's love for the lepers. He made their beds, tidied their rooms, and rebuilt their huts. He washed their bodies, bandaged their wounds, and anointed them with oil. When they were dying, he heard their confession, prayed for their salvation, and assured them of a decent burial.

> *'I make myself a leper with the lepers to gain all for Jesus Christ.'*
> — Damien

Damien did not see the lepers as helpless, and he recruited as many as he could as his partners to help him in his work. He taught them to till the soil and tend the animals. Together they built cottages for themselves and a home for their children. They made a road from the settlement at Kalawao to the shoreline at Kalaupapa, where they blasted the rocks and built a dock. They restored the church, learnt to play musical instruments, and sang jubilant songs to God — as only the Hawaiians can!

Meanwhile, Damien found himself fighting battles for the welfare of the lepers on three fronts. He clashed with the lepers who hung out at 'the crazy pen'. They not only refused to help, but steadfastly opposed his plans. He quarrelled with the government authorities, who rejected his constant demands for more resources. And he argued with his religious superiors, who were enraged by his willingness to go public in his appeal for the aid they withheld, without due regard for the embarrassment he caused the Church. He was constantly criticised, but Damien was undeterred in his commitment.

To begin with, Damien maintained a safe distance in his dealings with the lepers. But as time went by, Damien flung caution to the winds and embraced his leper friends physically, fully, freely, and without reservation. In December 1884, Damien was soaking his feet in hot water, but didn't feel the heat. Through his contact with the lepers, he had become a leper himself. He wrote to his brother saying: 'I make myself a leper with the lepers to gain all for Jesus Christ.' The lepers of Molokai gathered round the priest who had become one of them, and St Philomena's crowded chapel resounded with the joyful music of the choir, whose buoyant voices sang against the scourge of leprosy that attacked their vocal chords.

But while the lepers cherished him, his colleagues ostracised him. Some accused him of contracting leprosy as a result of getting syphilis 'by fornicating with lepers'. He declared his innocence, and submitted to a physical examination to prove to his detractors that he didn't have syphilis. But the scorn meted out by his order was a bitter blow —

the disdain, not the disease, being 'the greatest suffering he had ever endured in his life.'

Damien The Leper died on 15 April 1889 — just before Easter.

Molokai, a brilliant film on the life of Damien by Australian Director Paul Cox, is available on video/DVD. Get hold of it and watch it. You won't regret it; it is one of the most challenging movies ever made.

Suggestions for Meditation:

» What aspect of this story did you relate to most?
» Which be-attitude do you feel Joseph embodied best?
» What is the most valuable lesson you can learn from this story?

Remember Jesus said:

'Whatever you did
for one of the least of these brothers (and sisters) of mine,
you did for me.'

Matthew 25:40

MARY MACKILLOP

A Fair Dinkum Aussie Saint

Mary MacKillop was born in Fitzroy in 1842 into a Scottish migrant family.

Mary was the eldest of eight children, and their father — who had attended Scots College in Rome — educated the children at home.

Having squandered most of the family fortune, the MacKillops were dirt poor. So at the age of fourteen, Mary was sent out to work. By the age of sixteen, Mary had become the major family bread-winner.

Even in her youth, Mary showed herself to be a very capable person. At Sands & Kenny, the stationers where she worked, Mary was given a position of responsibility usually reserved for older employees.

At the age of eighteen Mary assumed the role of governess to her cousins in Penola, South Australia. There she met Father Julian Tenison Woods. Mary had already decided that she wanted to be a nun, so she asked Father Woods to be her spiritual mentor.

Julian Woods and Mary MacKillop became close friends. They shared a vision for developing an Australian religious order that would serve the needs of the poor.

In 1866, they founded 'The Sisters Of St. Joseph' — an indigenous mission, made up of small, mobile communities of two or three sisters, caring for kids in frontier towns, rural farms, and roadside and railway camps.

The itinerant lifestyle of the sisters was very simple. They took a vow of poverty to identify with the poor. And because they had no money, they were only able to get by through begging. The hierarchy of the church did not approve of the practice, but, mindful of her mission, Mary encouraged the sisters to carry on regardless.

Mary started Australia's first free Catholic school. At the time, only the rich could afford to pay the fees to send their kids to school. But the sisters provided education for the children of the poor — whether they could afford to pay the fees or not.

In 1867, Mary moved to Adelaide. And it wasn't long before she and her sisters had seventeen schools up and running. Instead of supporting their efforts, the Bishop of Adelaide tried to clamp down on the congregation. And when Mary resisted, he excommunicated her, and discharged her sisters.

For Mary, being thrown out of the church was a terrible blow. She was totally devastated. But, in spite of the desolation, she was determined to maintain her faith. She refused to become bitter and twisted about the way she was treated.

The Holy See sent a delegation to investigate the disturbance in the antipodes; and as a result of their enquiries, they decided to back Mary against the Bishop.

In 1872, when the Bishop lay dying, he apologized to Mary, absolved her from excommunication, and reinstated her and her sisters.

> *'Never see a need without trying to do something about it!'*
> — Mary MacKillop

In 1873, Mary travelled to Rome. There she sought permission from the Pope for her congregation to run its own affairs, free from the interference of the bishops in future. In the light of the quality of her work, her request was well received, and the Josephites were given the independence Mary had fought for.

In 1875, Mary was elected superior-general of her order.

Under Mary's guidance the Josephites became the primary provider of Catholic education to Australian girls — regardless of race, class or creed. And, because they had a policy of being non-proselytizing, the sisters enjoyed a lot of support from Protestants, as well as Catholics, in the communities where they worked around Australia.

In 1885, the Josephites found themselves in conflict with the bishops again. The Holy See supported the congregation, but asked Mary if she would stand aside and let someone else (less controversial) lead the congregation for a while.

So in 1888, Mary stood aside, and Mother Bernard was elected to lead the order in her stead. But in 1898 Mother Bernard died; Mary was elected again by the congregation to lead the order into the twentieth century.

They not only taught students, but also taught the teachers who taught the students. They opened orphanages for those with no homes, and refuges for those fleeing violent homes. And they provided family support services and residential care services for those with intellectual, physical, psychological and developmental disabilities.

In 1909, Mary died. And in 1995 this little battler, this feminist trailblazer and ecclesiastical troublemaker, this extraordinary never-say-die pioneer of education for all was recognized as our first fair dinkum Aussie Saint.

Suggestions for Meditation:
- » What aspect of this story did you relate to most?
- » Which be-attitude do you feel Mary embodied best?
- » What is the most valuable lesson you can learn from this story?

Remember Jesus said:
'In this world you will have trouble.
But take heart! I have overcome the world.' *John 16:33*

JOHN GRIBBLE

'The Black Fellow's Friend'

John Gribble was born in England in 1847. His parents, Benjamin and Mary, brought him to Australia in 1848 and he grew up in Geelong.

On one occasion during his childhood John got lost, and was found by an old Aboriginal woman who cared for him in the local Aboriginal camp. He never forgot their kindness, and sought to reciprocate it as much as he could.

When he was fourteen John was converted, and later studied to become a minister. At the age of twenty-one John married Mary-Anne, and they moved to Jerilderie where John was appointed as a minister. It was here that John encountered Ned Kelly.

One of the Kelly gang stole a young girl's horse. Gribble rode out after the gang, confronted Kelly with the 'unmanly act' of stealing a young girl's horse, and demanded he give it back immediately. Kelly assured Gribble he would.

Later on, the same member of the Kelly gang robbed Gribble of his watch. Gribble strode into town, called Kelly out of the pub, and demanded his watch back. The two stared at each other, but Kelly relented and gave Gribble his watch back.

His confrontations with bushrangers taught John the importance of 'talking truth to power'; a vocation he took up, with a commitment to justice, seldom witnessed in this country.

John began visiting Aboriginal people in poverty-stricken fringe camps. He was appalled to find they 'were filled to overflowing with wants and woes'; a condition, that was 'most shocking to contemplate'.

But, contemplate it, he did. 'The flesh said, "Stay where you are; why impoverish your family?" But the spirit said, "Go and rescue the perishing! Go and build them a home in the wilderness."'

In 1873, Daniel Matthews set up a refuge for Aborigines at Maloga, and in 1880, Matthew helped John establish a similar ministry at Warangesda. They were the only safe havens in New South Wales to which Indigenous victims of colonial violence could turn.

However, John felt it wasn't good enough just to provide safe havens for 'black victims'; he needed to speak out — publicly — against 'white violence'.

So, in 1883, John went to England, where he published an exposé on the treatment of Aborigines in Australia. The book asserted that the idea of peaceful settlement was an illusion; the reality was that, from the earliest times, 'the blacks' were 'wrongly treated by the white man'; they were used — and abused — 'like wild beasts'!

> *'If I am to continue working as their missionary, it must be on the lines of justice and right to the Aborigines of this land, in opposition to the injustice and wrong-doing of unprincipled white men. This is my decision and by it I stand or fall.'*
> — John Gribble

On his return from England to Australia in 1885, John decided to take up work with Aborigines in North-West Western Australia under the auspices of the Anglican Church.

After arriving at Carnarvon, John visited the camps at the back of town, and acquainted himself with the grief of the local Aboriginal population. Aboriginal women were captured by settlers, kept in chains, and used as sex slaves. Aboriginal men were pressed into service, to work in the pearling or pastoral industry. They were 'ruled by fear, flogged, underfed, and unpaid'.

When John expressed his anger over these injustices, the locals petitioned the Bishop to withdraw his licence; shopkeepers refused to sell him provisions, and a sign was hung on the pub crying: 'Down with Gribble.'

John jumped aboard a ship going to Perth to get some help. But, on board, he was attacked by the other passengers and, when he got to Perth, he was attacked on every side: by the public, the state, and the Church. The Bishop issued an 'unqualified condemnation' of the priest, and asserted the right, as his superior, to censor him.

John refused to capitulate and continued to write reports for the Aboriginal Protection Society. And the Daily Telegraph wrote a series of articles on 'Slavery In Western Australia' based on John's reports.

John was hounded out of Western Australia.

On his return to New South Wales, Daniel encouraged John to set up a safe haven in Far North Queensland where violence against Aborigines continued unabated.

In 1892, John cashed in his life assurance policies and moved to Cape Grafton, south of Cairns, where he purchased some land and set up Yarrabah as a safe haven for Aborigines.

In 1893, suffering from the effects of tuberculosis, malaria, and dengue fever, John Gribble died. He was forty-five. His tombstone reads: 'The Black Fellow's Friend'.

Suggestions for Meditation:
» What aspect of this story did you relate to most?
» Which be-attitude do you feel John embodied best?
» What is the most valuable lesson you can learn from this story?

Remember Jesus said:
'If you belonged to the world, it would love you as its own.
But you do not belong to the world. That is why the world hates you.'
John 15:19

PANDITA RAMABAI

The Learned One

Ramabai was born into a high-caste Brahmin family in Maharashtra in 1858. Her family were very devout Hindus and often took the young Ramabai on pilgrimage to holy places — climbing up sacred mountains, bathing in sacred rivers, and visiting temples all over India. At the time it was the practice not to teach women Sanskrit, India's classical language, or the Vedas, India's classical philosophy. But Ramabai's father considered this custom discriminatory, and, in total defiance of tradition, taught both his wife and his children, including Ramabai, the secret wisdom of India.

Then came the first in a series of disasters that was to be a defining moment in Ramabai's life. The famine of 1876 killed everyone in Ramabai's family, except her and one of her brothers.

On his deathbed, her father held Ramabai in his arms and said to her: 'Remember how I loved you. Serve God always. I leave you in His keeping.'

In 1878, at the age of twenty, Ramabai went to Calcutta with her brother to look for work. It was a fortuitous decision. For, of all the learned cities of India, Calcutta celebrated learning like no other, and it wasn't very long before the whole city was talking about the erudite young scholar they lovingly called 'Pandita', the 'Learned One'.

During her time in Calcutta the much-loved Pandita Ramabai got married, bore a daughter and began a major campaign for women's education. Then came the second disaster that was to define Ramabai's life. In an outbreak of cholera that periodically swept through the city of Calcutta, Ramabai's husband suddenly took sick and died. So after only nineteen brief months of marriage, Ramabai was left alone once more.

As she began to ponder her predicament, firstly as an orphan, and secondly as a widow, Ramabai was forced to face the terrible plight of other orphans and widows. And she was determined that she would do whatever she could to help them.

In order to get the training she felt that she needed to move from scholarship to social work, Ramabai travelled to England, where she went to Cheltenham Ladies College and got involved with the Wantage Sisters, a community of Christian women who worked with prostitutes.

'I had never heard or seen anything (like) this before,' Ramabai wrote. '(And) my heart was drawn to the religion of Christ.'

In 1889, Ramabai returned to India as a devout Christian and founded a home in Mumbai for abandoned Brahmin widows and orphans like herself. It was a controversial venture. Nothing like it had ever been done before. But it proved such a success that many other groups began to provide similar services for needy people in their communities.

> *'My heart was drawn to the religion of Christ.'*
> —Pandita Ramabai

Then came the third in the series of disasters that was to be a defining moment in Ramabai's life. The famine of 1896 made the famine in 1876 look like a picnic. Millions of people all over India died like flies.

In the face of this catastrophe Ramabai felt called to extend her care across caste boundaries, beyond just helping Brahmin widows and orphans like herself to helping all widows and all orphans, regardless of their caste.

So she set up the Mukti Mission and, without so much as a rupee in promised funds to her name, threw open the doors of her mission to help as many people as she could. By 1900, her Mukti Mission was responsible for the welfare of some 1,900 widows and orphans!

Over the ensuing years the 'Learned One' developed a legendary reputation for tireless evangelism, education and emancipation. 'I am busy from 4:30 in the morning till 8:30 at night. Till my feet are aching and my head is tired,' she once said. 'What a blessing this burden does not fall on me. But Christ bears it on his shoulders.'

In 1922, Pandita Ramabai died, but her vision and her work live on.

Suggestions for Meditation:
» What aspect of this story did you relate to most?
» Which be-attitude do you feel Ramabai embodied best?
» What is the most valuable lesson you can learn from this story?

Remember Jesus said:
'In this world you will have trouble.
But take heart! I have overcome the world.' *John 16:33*

C.F. ANDREWS

Christ's Faithful Apostle

Charles Freer Andrews was born in 1871 in Newcastle, England. He was the fourth child in a family of twelve. He had a particularly close relationship with his mother who nursed him through a prolonged period of illness.

In 1877, the family moved to Birmingham where Charlie's father was called to be a minister in the charismatic Catholic Apostolic Church. Through his father's 'long round of spiritual toil' with the battlers in the big grimy industrial town, Charlie's father taught him two things — a love for prayer and a love for the poor.

While Charlie was still quite young, his mother lost all her money through the duplicity of a family friend, and the family were plunged into poverty themselves. But his parents' response to the disaster made an indelible impression on young Charlie. On the night they got the news of their ruin, his parents quietly gathered the family together and prayed for forgiveness for the man who had ruined them. And, from then on, Charlie watched his parents work and scrimp and save 'untiringly all day long' for the sake of their children. Later, he was to say of his mother: 'Her pure unselfishness made us ashamed...to act in self-indulgent ways.'

Charlie studied at the King Edward VI School in Birmingham. In 1890, just before he was due to start his study in Classics at Pembroke College, Cambridge, Charlie had a personal encounter with Christ that was to prove to be the turning point of his life. In 1896, Charlie became a deacon, and took over the Pembroke College Mission in South London. Then in 1897, he became a priest, and three years later took on the work of Vice-Principal of Westcott House Theological College in Cambridge.

While at college, Charlie became involved in the Christian Social Union, and began to explore the relationship between a commitment to the gospel and a commitment to justice. He became increasingly interested in the struggle for justice throughout the empire, in India in particular. So in 1904, when Charlie was invited to join the Cambridge Brotherhood as a teacher at St Stephen's College in Delhi, he jumped at the chance to go.

Charlie was quite shocked with the racist attitudes of the British in India. He felt an immediate rapport with the Indians he met, who were trying to reform Hinduism and struggling to create a modern independent Indian state. In 1906, Charlie decided to go public with his opinions — writing a letter, published in the *Civil and Military Gazette*, Lahore, openly supporting the Indian nationalists.

As a British supporter of an independent India, Charlie was in a special position. He was invited to attend meetings of the Indian National Congress, and he was trusted by both the British and the Indians to be an intermediary. In 1913, Charlie successfully intervened in the Madras cotton workers' strike. Later that year, Gokhale, the leader of the Congress, asked Charlie to go to South Africa to help the Indian community there resolve some of their difficulties with the British authorities. By all reports, he did this very expeditiously.

While in South Africa, Charlie met Mahatma Gandhi. Upon their return to India, Charlie worked very closely with Gandhi, the Congress and the Unions. In 1925 and 1927, Charlie was elected the President of the All India Trade Union. And from 1931 to 1932, Charlie sat beside Gandhi at the Round Table Conference, and helped him negotiate with the British Government on behalf of the Indian National Congress.

While working for independence for India, Charlie developed a dialogue between Christians and Hindus. He spent a lot of time at *Shantiniketan Ashram* in conversation with the poet philosopher Rabindranath Tagore. He also supported the movement to ban the 'untouchability of outcastes'. In 1925, he joined the famous Vaikkom Temple Protests, and in 1933, he assisted Dr. Ambedkar in formulating Harijan ('untouchables') demands.

About this time, Gandhi took Charlie aside and told him that it was probably best for sympathetic Britishers like himself to leave the Indian independence movement to the Indians. So from 1935 onwards, Charlie began to spend more time back in Britain, teaching young people all over the country about Christ's call to radical discipleship. Over time, C.F. Andrews became affectionately known as 'Christ's Faithful Apostle'.

On 5 April 1940, Charlie died and was buried while on a visit to Calcutta.

Charlie and Mohan — Friendship As Partnership

Charlie Andrews was said to be the only man who called the great Mahatma Gandhi 'Mohan.'
When Charlie first met the Mahatma in South Africa, Mohandas Gandhi had just been released from prison for organising a campaign of non-violent protest against the government. Instinctively, Charlie stooped and, in a traditional Indian sign of respect, touched Gandhi's feet. The South Africans were mortified. 'We don't do that sort of thing in Natal,' they said. But from that moment, Charlie and Mohan were lifelong friends.
There were a number of features of his friendship with Charlie that Gandhi loved. He loved Charlie. Gandhi said: 'I have not known a better man than C.F. Andrews.' He loved the special relationship he had with Charlie. 'Nobody knew Charlie Andrews as well as I did.' It was close. 'There was no distance between us.' It bridged the vast chasm of culture, tradition and religion. 'He was a son of England who also became a son of India. And he did it all for the sake of his Lord and Master Jesus Christ.' Their friendship could bear the weight of honest debate. Gandhi once wrote to Horace Alexander, 'I want you to criticize me as frankly and fearlessly as Charlie!' It was equal, mutual and respectful. 'When we met, we simply met as brothers and remained as such to the end. Our friendship was an unbreakable bond between two seekers and servants.'
Charlie did all he could to help Mohan in his struggle and, in return, Mohan cared for Charlie — nursing him personally while he was ill in Calcutta and holding his hand himself during the last few days of his life.

Suggestions for Meditation:
- » What aspect of this story did you relate to most?
- » Which be-attitude do you feel Charlie embodied best?
- » What is the most valuable lesson you can learn from this story?

Remember Jesus said:

'A good tree bears good fruit, but a bad tree bears bad fruit. Thus, by their fruit you will recognize them.' *Matthew 7:20*

HELEN KELLER

The Light in the Darkness

Helen Keller was born on 27 July 1880 in Tuscumbia, Alabama, in the United States. She was a healthy newborn, but at 19 months of age a fever left her blind and deaf.

Her father Arthur (an ex-confederate captain) and her mother Kate (a southern socialite) didn't know what to do with their daughter. Helen's frustration at not being able to communicate made her angry. She would smash dishes at the dinner table and oil lamps round the family home, 'terrorizing the whole household with her temper tantrums'. Relatives advised them to put 'the little monster in an institution'.

By the time Helen was six years old, her parents were desperate. They consulted a local expert — Alexander Graham Bell, the inventor of the telephone. He was also an activist in education for the deaf. Bell counselled the Kellers to find a teacher for Helen as soon as possible.

The Perkins School for the Blind recommended a recent graduate by the name of Anne Sullivan. On 3 March 1887, Anne came to serve as Helen's governess. She moved with Helen into a small cottage on the Keller's property, and started Helen's education.

Anne taught Helen to finger-spell. Anne had bought Helen a doll, and taught her to spell out the word 'doll.' Helen's behaviour was abominable. Anne refused to 'talk' with her if she didn't behave properly. Helen's behaviour improved markedly. In a matter of weeks, a real bond developed between them.

Then the 'miracle' occurred. Anne took Helen to the water pump, poured water over her hands, and spelled out 'water'. Until then, Helen had not really understood the meaning of words, but at that moment, she says, she got it. 'The mystery of language was revealed to me.' She wanted to spell out the whole world.

From then on, Helen's progress was amazing. It wasn't long before Anne was teaching Helen to read. She learnt to read and write in Braille. She even learnt to type on an ordinary typewriter. 'Her ability to learn was far in advance of anything that anybody had seen before in someone without sight or hearing,' recalled Anne. She became a celebrity. Pictures of Helen reading Shakespeare appeared in the national press.

In 1890, Anne took Helen with her to the Perkins Institute to continue her education. In the hope of learning to speak, Helen went with Anne to the Wright-Humason School of the Deaf in New York City in 1894. Because her vocal chords were underdeveloped, Helen was never able to speak clearly. However, she was still able to go to college and, in 1900, she became the first deaf-blind person to ever enroll in tertiary education. In 1904, Helen graduated from Radcliffe College, the first deaf-blind person to earn a Bachelor of Arts degree.

In 1913, Helen published *Out Of The Dark*, a series of essays on social justice. 'When indeed shall we learn we are all related one to the other, we are all members of one body?' she wrote. 'Until the great mass of the people shall be filled with the sense of responsibility for each other's welfare, social justice can never be attained.'

Helen practised what she preached. She spent most of her time helping others, particularly the poor. She wrote tirelessly, advocating on behalf of people with disabilities. When the American Foundation for the Blind was organized in 1921, Helen gladly became their global ambassador. She worked in that role for the rest of her life.

Helen was a woman of strong faith, who could honestly say: 'I thank God for my handicaps, for through them, I have found myself, my work and my God.'

She died on 1 June 1968.

> *'Unless we form the habit of going to the Bible in bright moments as well as in trouble, we cannot fully respond to its consolations because we lack equilibrium between light and darkness. Faith is the strength by which a shattered world shall emerge into the light.'* — Helen Keller

The Elderly Nurse

When Queen Victoria asked Helen how she was able to do so much, Helen said she owed it all to Anne.
Anne's story is almost as remarkable as Helen's. Due to a childhood fever, Anne was almost blind. As an angry, frustrated child, Anne was diagnosed as 'insane' and locked in the basement of a mental institution. Hearing about this 'hopeless case', an elderly nurse began to visit her. Anne rejected her overtures, but the nurse refused to give up. She responded in kindness, with cookies. Eventually, Anne's life was transformed by her love. Anne grew up with the resolve to show the same quality of care that this elderly nurse had shown to her. The rest is history.

Suggestions for Meditation:

» What aspect of this story did you relate to most?
» Which be-attitude do you feel Helen embodied best?
» What is the most valuable lesson you can learn from this story?

Remember Jesus said:

'Let your light shine before people,
 that they may see your good deeds and praise your Father in heaven.'
Matthew 5:16

TOYOHIKO KAGAWA

A Love-Intoxicated Personality

Toyohiko Kagawa was born in 1888, the son of a rich Japanese businessman and one of his many concubines. By the time he had turned just four years of age, Toyohiko had lost both parents and was left all alone.

The Buddhist orphan was cared for by some Presbyterian missionaries, and so came to learn about the love of Christ. At the age of fifteen Toyohiko was baptised, and began intently studying Christian pacifist classics, such as *The Kingdom Of God* by Leo Tolstoy, the famous author of *War and Peace*.

At the age of sixteen Toyohiko went to Tokyo to study theology. At that time Japan was at war with Russia, and the young peace activist spoke out publicly against it, much to the dismay of fellow students who were embarrassed about his protests. They put him on trial for treason, and, adjudging him guilty, beat him mercilessly. Needless to say Toyohiko became increasingly disillusioned with the kind of Christianity that he encountered at seminary. He said that he yearned for 'a gospel incarnated' in what he called 'love-intoxicated personalities' and 'demonstrated in institutions which sacrifice and serve.' He cried, '(We) must show what Christian ideals actually mean!'

On Christmas Day 1909, Toyohiko Kagawa, aged twenty-one, walked out of the seminary, and, with his few simple belongings packed in a handcart, made his way to the slums of Shinkawa, which were to become his home for the next fifteen years.

Toyohiko poured himself out for the poor: visiting the lonely, feeding the hungry, comforting the bereaved, accommodating as many of the homeless in his own little hut as he could...even when he got married! But Toyohiko not only worked for the poor – Toyohiko worked with the poor: practising gospel processes, developing cooperative societies, organising peasant unions, contributing to the labour movement in the establishment of the Labor Party. Toyohiko was a twentieth century polymath. His writings encompassed the entire breadth and depth of the human experience that he sought to embrace. He wrote a six hundred and fifty-four page study, *On the Psychology of the Poor*, and his 1920 autobiographical novel, *Crossing The Death Line*, became a huge best seller in Japan. Typically, Toyohiko reinvested the royalties from his books in his work.

In 1923, when an earthquake wrecked Tokyo, the government turned to the incorruptible Toyohiko to supervise relief and reconstruction in the city. Toyohiko agreed. On one condition — that he would take no pay! In 1928, in the shadow of war, Toyohiko set up the All-Japan Anti-War League. In 1938, Kagawa met Gandhi, and with Einstein, they put their signatures to a famous international Anti-War Pact. Not surprisingly, in 1940 Toyohiko's magazine, *The Pillar Of Cloud,* was banned, and Toyohiko himself was put in prison. Bills were posted round Tokyo calling for Toyohiko's execution. 'Kill the traitor Kagawa!' they screamed. 'He is a traitor to the nation!' Somehow Toyohiko survived. And as soon as he got out of custody he made a visit to America in a last ditch effort to avert the oncoming war with Japan. 'When nations engage in war,' Toyohiko warned, 'they become brutal!' Back in Japan after the war began, Toyohiko was in and out of jail, but he continued his anti-war activities. He even made a special trip to China, to the China National Christian Council, where he personally apologised to the Chinese for the Japanese Rape Of Nanking.

> *'Christ alone can make all things new. The spirit of Christ must be the soul of all real social reconstruction.'*
> — Toyohiko Kagawa

In 1945, after the war was over, Toyohiko was appointed as an advisor to the Prime Minister. He was made the Commissioner for National Social Welfare, and one of the first things he did was call for a Campaign Of National Repentance.

'Christ alone can make all things new,' Toyohiko said. 'The spirit of Christ must be the soul of all real social reconstruction.' When Rabbi Israel Goldstein, the president of the American Jewish Congress, was asked if he could name a Christian who could work together with Jews for world peace, without hesitation he nominated Toyohiko Kagawa, saying that his 'religion is contagious'. In recognition of his ongoing commitment to world peace, Toyohiko was elected the President of the All-Asian Congress for World Federation, and the Vice-President of the Union for World Federal Government. On 25 April 1960, Toyohiko Kagawa died.

Suggestions for Meditation:
» What aspect of this story did you relate to most?
» Which be-attitude do you feel Toyohiko embodied best?
» What is the most valuable lesson you can learn from this story?

Remember Jesus said:
'God is spirit,
 and his worshippers must worship in spirit and in truth.' *John 4:24*

DOROTHY DAY

The Woman Who Wanted To Change the World

Dorothy Day was born in Brooklyn in 1897. Her father was unemployed, and so in 1906 her family had to move into a poor tenement flat in the South Side of Chicago. Dorothy said that her understanding of the plight of the poor dated from that point.

John Day eventually got a job as a sports writer for a Chicago newspaper, and the family moved into a comfortable house on the North Side. Even then Dorothy didn't forget the people living on the South Side, and used to take long walks through the derelict streets.

In 1914, Dorothy won a scholarship to study at the University of Illinois. But she proved to be more interested in reading radical social writers than studying prescribed courses.

Two years later, her family moved to New York, and Dorothy decided to go with them in order to pursue her dream of becoming a radical social writer herself. It wasn't long before Dorothy became a contributor to revolutionary papers like the *New Masses* and the *Call*. She wrote passionately on the subject of women's rights, free love and birth control.

In 1917, Dorothy joined a demonstration in front of the White House protesting the cruel treatment of suffragettes who were in prison. She got herself 30 days for her trouble.

At this stage of her life, Dorothy had a series of affairs, got pregnant, and had an abortion. On the rebound from one of her affairs, she got married. It only lasted a year. In 1926, Dorothy found herself pregnant again. But this time she was determined to keep the baby.

The birth of her baby proved to be a major spiritual turning point in Dorothy's life. As a child, she had attended church, and as a young journalist, she had gone to late-night mass.

After her abortion, Dorothy was medically unable to have any more children. She saw the birth of her child as a miracle. In gratitude, she wanted to dedicate her life — and the life of her child — to God.

However Foster Batterham, the father of the child, was a militant atheist and opposed the idea. Dorothy felt she was faced with a stark choice. Either to go along with her lover, or give up her lover for God. Dorothy chose what she was later to call 'the long loneliness' of living for God alone. On 18 December 1927, she broke off her relationship with Batterham, and Dorothy and her baby daughter, Tamar Teresa, were baptized.

Dorothy now set about the task of reworking her radical views in the light of her faith. She was helped in this process by Peter Maurin, a poetic French peasant and philosopher.

In May 1933, five months after meeting Peter, Dorothy put out the first edition of *The Catholic Worker*. It was a penny-a-copy monthly newspaper, committed to advocating the teachings of Christ with regard to the major social issues of the day.

Through *The Catholic Worker*, Dorothy promoted neutral pacifism during the Spanish Civil War (1936–1939). 'We were not, of course, pro-Franco, but followers of Gandhi in our struggle to build a spirit of non-violence. But in those days we got it from both sides; it was a holy war to most Catholics, just as world revolution is holy war to Communists,' she wrote.

> *'What we would like to do is change the world — make it a little simpler for people to feed, clothe, and shelter themselves as God intended them to do. And...by fighting for better conditions, by crying out unceasingly for the rights of the poor — the rights of the worthy and the unworthy poor — we can to a certain extent change the world.'* — Dorothy

The editorial policy of *The Catholic Worker* was based on a personalist philosophy, emphasising the importance of people accepting personal responsibility for the welfare of society. So it came as no surprise that *The Catholic Worker* community opened a House of Hospitality in the slums of New York. Its purpose was simply to practise those works that sound a good idea in theory, such as housing the homeless and feeding the hungry.

When the social revolution of the 1960s rolled round, Dorothy was hailed as the 'grand old lady of pacifism'. Crowds of 'wanna-be-revolutionaries' sought her out to ask for her advice. But they usually got more than they bargained for. Dorothy was uncompromising in her call for personal morality, voluntary poverty, radical hospitality and pro-life activism.

She explained: 'What we would like to do is change the world — make it a little simpler for people to feed, clothe, and shelter themselves as God intended them to do. And to a certain extent, by fighting for better conditions, by crying out unceasingly for the rights of the poor — the rights of the worthy and the unworthy poor — we can to a certain extent change the world.'

No other newspaper ever had more editors in prison for crying out unceasingly for the rights of the poor than *The Catholic Worker*. Dorothy herself was last imprisoned in 1973 for taking part in a banned picket line in support of farm labourers. She was 75.

Dorothy died seven years later, in 1980, aged 83. After a lifetime of voluntary poverty, she left no money for her funeral. It was paid for by the Archdiocese of New York.

At the end of Dorothy Day's life, everybody wanted to meet and talk with her. The steady flow of visitors…often tired her out. Some of the young volunteers…were most insistent. One day, several of them approached her, hoping to persuade her to join them in a big demonstration against nuclear weapons at the United Nations. Mass arrests were expected at the planned UN sit-in, and she guessed that the youthful activists were secretly wanting to tell their children one day that they had once been arrested with Dorothy Day. Dorothy, however, was quite unenthusiastic. 'I've done that enough times already; you go ahead without me,' she told them. 'Oh, please, Dorothy,' they replied. 'It would be such a great experience!' After their repeated efforts to change her mind, Dorothy finally said, 'Look, if I came along, here's what would happen. We would all be sitting in a circle, and the police would come. They would take all of you away and leave me for last because I'm so old. I'd be sitting there alone. Finally, the police would all be standing over me, shaking their heads, and asking, 'What are you doing here?' And I'd probably forget!'

From *Faith Works: Lessons on Spirituality and Social Action.*
Jim Wallis, SPCK, London, 2002.

Suggestions for Meditation:
» What aspect of this story did you relate to most?
» Which be-attitude do you feel Dorothy embodied best?
» What is the most valuable lesson you can learn from this story?

Remember Jesus said:
'Make disciples of all nations,
teaching them to obey everything I have commanded you.'
Matthew 28:19–20

ALBERT LUTHULI

The Apartheid Opponent

Albert Luthuli was probably born in 1898 in Groutville, Natal, South Africa.

His father died when Albert was six months old, so it was left to his mother, Mtonya, to bring up Albert by herself. Mtonya had spent her childhood in the Royal Kraal of King Cetewayo in Zululand, and felt it was her duty to raise her child with the courtly virtues of dignity and discipline. A devout Christian, Mtonya also raised her son Albert to be a committed Christian.

He trained as a teacher and was sent to teach at Blaauwbosch, in the Natal uplands. Though he could never pinpoint a date when he was 'converted', Albert was convinced that it was during his time in the Natal uplands, where he came under the influence of a very conscientious African Methodist, Rev. Mtembu, that he became much more serious about his faith.

After two years teaching Albert was offered a bursary to do a Higher Teacher Training at Adams College. On graduation he was appointed to the staff of the college, where he stayed for the next fifteen years. During this time he was profoundly influenced by C.W. Atkins, the Head of the Training College. Albert said of Atkins, 'He typifies for me the side of Adams that I found most valuable...He placed his emphasis on loving God and on service of society...and in involving us deeply in the affairs of African communities...'

In 1936, Albert was elected as Chief of the Umvoti Mission Reserve, which had its headquarters in his home town. He accepted the appointment reluctantly, knowing full well that the position would thrust him into the forefront of his people's struggle for human rights.

Two years later Albert travelled to Chennai, India, as a delegate to the World Missionary Conference. Here, as a black South African, he enjoyed the pleasure of eating, drinking, and conversing with whites as an equal for the first time in his life. On the flight home, because of his colour, he was consigned to second class while white South Africans travelled first class. Moreover, Albert was told in no uncertain terms by a Dutch Reformed minister that *he* was not welcome to join *them* in worship. Albert gagged on the indignity that *apartheid* dished out to him, and he vowed to fight it.

For the next ten years Albert fought for the right of subsistence farmers on the Umvoti Mission Reserve to own their own land. But 'rights' for the blacks were seen as 'privileges' by the whites, and those 'privileges' were slowly but surely being withdrawn.

After a visit to the USA in 1948, where he was inspired by the power of the civil rights movement to combat systemic racism, Albert joined the African National Congress (ANC) — 'to oppose a system — not a race'. It wasn't long before he was elected President of the ANC. As President, Albert coordinated the ANC Defiance Campaign, that defied government restrictions on the movement of blacks — these even prevented a 'black' wife from moving into a town to join her 'black' husband without the threat of being arrested by the 'white' police.

> *'He was a Christian, with very deeply held beliefs, (about) throwing the moneylenders out of the temple!'*
> — A friend of Albert's

The government reacted to the ANC Defiance Campaign with great fury. In 1952, Albert was deposed from his position, as Chief of the Umvoti Mission Reserve, and banned completely from being able to travel to any of the larger towns in South Africa.

Despite a stroke in 1955, Albert still managed to help organize the great 'Congress of the People'. Invoking its anti-communist legislation, the government arrested twenty thousand congress sympathisers and charged Albert with High Treason.

After the trial things got worse. The Pass Laws — enacted by the minority white government to control the majority black population — were tightened up, and all opposition to the Pass Laws was prohibited.

In 1960, the ANC was banned. And Albert was banned from meeting more than one person at a time. His response was to publicly lead his people in burning their pass cards.

Albert also argued very strongly for economic sanctions against South Africa, on the grounds that he thought they were the only chance of a 'relatively peaceful transition' for the country.

For most of his active political life Albert favoured a non-violent struggle against *apartheid*, but he was not a pacifist, saying that 'anyone who thought he was should try to steal his chickens!' However, in 1961, Albert was awarded the Nobel Peace Prize for his non-violent struggle against *apartheid* in South Africa.

On his death in 1967, it was said of Albert Luthuli that he 'possessed a remarkable generosity of spirit, but was never tolerant of injustice. He was a Christian, with very deeply held beliefs, but of the kind that looked for its example in throwing the moneylenders out of the temple!'

Suggestions for Meditation:
» What aspect of this story did you relate to most?
» Which be-attitude do you feel Albert embodied best?
» What is the most valuable lesson you can learn from this story?

Remember Jesus said:
'When they arrest you, do not worry about what to say or how to say it. At that time you will be given what to say, for it will not be you speaking, but the Spirit speaking through you.' *Matthew 10:19–20*

DIETRICH BONHOEFFER

The Man Who Stood By God

In 1906, Dietrich Bonhoeffer was born into a very respectable family in Breslau.

When he was six, Dietrich's father was appointed as Director of the Psychiatric Clinic at the University of Berlin. So Dietrich grew up in the capital of Germany.

Dietrich's great-grandfather was Karl von Hase, a famous Protestant Professor of Church History in Jena, and Dietrich was brought up as a dutiful young Lutheran. His family were probably actually more Prussian than they were Protestant, but Dietrich developed a passion for religion that transcended his devotion to tradition.

Of the eight Bonhoeffer children, Dietrich was the only one who decided that he wanted to study theology. And study theology he did.

To begin with Dietrich went to the illustrious University in Tübingen, then came back to Berlin. Later he went to the celebrated Union Theological Seminary in New York.

Dietrich was very much influenced by the ideas of the world-renowned German Protestant theologian Karl Barth, whose series of lectures he had attended as a student.

Dietrich was a theological prodigy. Barth himself commended his early brilliant academic work. So it was hardly surprising that the theological whizz kid was appointed as a lecturer in theology at the University of Berlin at a very young age.

From 1933 to 1935, Dietrich served as a pastor for two German speaking churches in London. During this time he formed a close friendship with Bishop Bell of Chichester.

Dietrich told him of his fears about the rise of the Nazi Party in Germany. He was particularly worried about the fact that so many German Christians seemed to embrace Hitler as some kind of messianic figure who would save German Christianity.

Dietrich had already joined the Confessing Church that opposed the Nazi Party. But he felt the Confessing Church did not go far enough. He had begun to speak out against the persecution of the Jews. But try as he might, he could not get the Confessing Church to support his protests.

The Bishop affirmed Bonhoeffer, and as the leader of the Ecumenical Movement, promised the young activist the wholehearted support of his organisation for the struggle.

In 1935, Dietrich returned to Germany to start a theological seminary under the auspices of the Confessing Church. In 1937, the government shut down the subversive Finkenwalde Centre, but Dietrich continued to train his students underground.

In 1939, Dietrich was called up for military service. He refused to take an oath of loyalty to the Führer, and found himself in a head-on confrontation with the authorities.

Reinhold Niebuhr, the American theologian, invited Dietrich to New York to deliver a series of lectures. When war was declared Dietrich was tempted to stay on, but he felt constrained by God to cut short his stay in the US, and return home to Germany to face the future — for better or worse — with his people.

When he arrived home, his brother-in-law Hans von Dohnanyi invited Dietrich to join the resistance movement that was conspiring to bring down the Nazi Party and put Hitler on trial.

For years he worked for the Abwehr, against the Gestapo — passing on information to the allies through Bishop Bell, whom he met in Sweden, and smuggling Jews out of Germany into Switzerland.

In 1943, Dietrich was arrested and charged with 'subversion of the armed forces' — for encouraging students not to do military service.

Though a pacifist, Dietrich eventually came to the conclusion that the only way they could bring the Nazi Party down and end the madness — was to assassinate Hitler.

So Dietrich got involved in von Stauffenberg's famous attempt to blow up the Fuhrer. It failed. And Dietrich, along with his co-conspirators, was sentenced to death.

On 9 April 1945, Dietrich Bonhoeffer was executed. He had sought to 'stand by God in his agony.'

> All go to God in their distress,
> seek help and pray for bread and happiness.
> (But) Christians stand by God in his agony.
> All go to God in their distress,
> seek help and pray for bread and happiness,
> deliverance from pain, guilt and death.
> All do, Christians and others.

All go to God in His distress,
find him poor, reviled without help or bread
watch him tormented by sin, weakness and death.
Christians stand by God in his agony.
— *Dietrich*

Suggestions for Meditation:

» What aspect of this story did you relate to most?
» Which be-attitude do you feel Dietrich embodied best?
» What is the most valuable lesson you can learn from this story?

Remember Jesus said:

'If anyone would come after me,
they must deny themselves and take up their cross and follow me.'
Matthew 16:24

SIMONE WEIL

'The Red Virgin'

Simone Weil was born in Paris, on 3 February 1909, into an affluent Jewish family.

Her elder brother André made sure that she received the very best education. And Simone, a precocious student, made the most of her opportunity, graduating with almost perfect marks in 1924, at the age of fifteen.

In 1928, she began her study in philosophy, fascinated by mathematics and mysticism; and, in 1931, was appointed as a teacher of philosophy at a secondary school for girls in Puy.

Simone was determined that she would never be an ivory tower academic, so right from the start the so-called 'Vierge Rouge', or 'Red Virgin', combined her growing interest in radicalism with a growing personal involvement in the plight of the poor.

'I have the need to move among (them),' she wrote, 'mixing with them, and sharing their life…so as to love them just as they are.'

To begin with Simone visited people, listening to their stories, and telling others of their concerns through a local journal. But upon reflection, Simone felt that this was pretty superficial, so she decided to take a year's leave from her privileged position at school to immerse herself as fully as she could in the life of the poor.

She took a job as an unskilled labourer, then as a milling machine operator for the car manufacturer Renault, moving into a small room near the factory, and living at the same standard of living as her companions in the workshop. Since childhood Simone had suffered from severe headaches, and she found the excruciating level of physical exertion and psychological stress that went with being a wage slave almost unbearable. But she stayed with it till the end of the year.

The next year she returned to teaching philosophy, but during the summer holidays Simone took time out to spend a few weeks on the front line with the republicans who were fighting for their lives against the fascists in Spain. For someone with a well-developed sensibility, like Simone, the afflictions of war were appalling.

It 'makes God appear absent, more absent than (the) dead,' she said. 'A kind of horror submerges the whole soul. If the soul stops loving, it falls into something which is almost the equivalent to hell'.

Soon the war was to engulf France. In 1940, Simone, with her Jewish family, fled the advancing German invasion.

While in southern France, Simone met a Dominican priest by the name of Perrin. The two became good friends. Perrin encouraged Simone, who said 'I always adopted a Christian attitude', to become more explicit in her implicit love for Christ. And she says that as she prayed, 'Christ himself came and took possession of me'. As a consequence of this experience Simone plunged herself more deeply into the work of the resistance, which was for her, 'Christian love for one's neighbour.'

> *'Disowning Christ (means) not being ready to die out of loyalty to him.'*
> —Simone

In 1942, Perrin was arrested by the Gestapo, and Simone fled to America. But she didn't stay there long. She was called upon to serve the French Government in exile, and went to England to work for them.

Simone was commissioned to write a document on the reciprocal rights and responsibilities of the citizen and the state, later published as *The Need For Roots*.

In 1943, Simone died. An illness from which she was suffering was apparently aggravated by her refusal to eat anything more than was available to her compatriots in occupied France.

Suggestions for Meditation:
» What aspect of this story did you relate to most?
» Which be-attitude do you feel Simone embodied best?
» What is the most valuable lesson you can learn from this story?

Remember Jesus said:
'Whoever wants to save their life will lose it,
but whoever loses their life for me will find it.' *Matthew 16:25*

DOM HELDER CAMARA

'The Red Bishop'

Helder Camara was born in 1909 in Fortaleza in the north-east of Brazil. He was the eleventh son in a family of thirteen children, almost half of whom died of the flu. His father, Joao, was a guard in a local company and his mother, Adelaide, was a teacher. His father was not religious, but the young Helder was very much influenced by an order of priests who served in his home town. By the age of four, Helder was 'playing church' and saying he wanted to be 'a Lazarus Priest' when he grew up.

In 1917, Helder took his first communion, and in 1923 entered the Diocesan Seminary. There he studied philosophy and theology, and developed his formidable debating skills. In 1931, at the age of 22, Helder was ordained a priest. At his ordination, he was commissioned to 'speak for humble people'. This call was to become his vocation.

Helder was sent to Ceara. Right from the start of his ministry, he advocated human rights. He immediately set up a Legion of Work for men in his region. Two years later, with the help of some local maids, he set up the Organisation of Feminine Labour for women.

For Helder, education was a critical component of both formation and transformation. So, just like his mother, he launched himself into teaching and training teachers, a task at which he excelled so much that he was invited to be State Director of Public Instruction.

In 1936, Helder moved to Rio de Janeiro, where he took up the position of Director of the Teaching of Religion, and worked to reform the teaching of religion in the state education system. After some time he became editor of a magazine called 'Catholic Action.'

In 1952, Helder became auxiliary bishop in the diocese of Rio de Janeiro where, three years later, he became auxiliary archbishop. At the same time, he founded the National Bishops Conference of Brazil, and developed the General Conference of the Latin-American Bishopric for the foundation of the Latin-American Episcopal Council (CELAM).

Over the next 12 years, Helder became more and more personally involved in the struggle of the people living in the favellas, the slums in Rio de Janeiro, and used his position as vice-president of the Latin-American Episcopal Council to advocate on behalf of the poor.

In 1964, Helder was appointed Bishop of Olinda and Recife, back in the north-east of Brazil where he had originally come from – one of the poorest parts of the country. So he moved into a couple of rooms at the back of a church in downtown Pernambuco. Within a few days of taking up his office, there was a military coup in Brazil. The democratic government was overthrown and many of the leaders of Catholic Action were thrown into prison, along with members of congress, union organisers, and journalists.

Helder spoke out against what he called the 'reign of terror'. When questioned about his courageous stand, he answered testily: 'I am trying to send men to heaven, not sheep. And certainly not sheep with their stomachs empty, and their testicles crushed.'

The military promptly branded him 'The Red Bishop'. But Helder replied — in a famous statement that was picked up, passed on, and copied endlessly, until it cried out from notice boards in community households all over the world: 'When I feed the poor, they call me a saint. When I ask why the poor have no food, they call me a communist!' Helder always insisted he was a Christian, not a Marxist.

Helder worked on preparations for the Second Vatican Council (Vatican II) which ran from 1962 to 1964, and which introduced the greatest range of reforms in the church since the Protestant Reformation, including base ecclesial communities.

Helder was only five feet tall, but during the 1970s he became a huge beacon of hope for people around the world who supported a radically compassionate spirituality, and opposed oppressive political structures, both secular and religious.

In 1985, Dom Helder Camara retired. He died in 1999, at the age of ninety.

Helder Camara used to get up in the middle of the night to pray, a habit dating from his time in seminary. During his nightly vigils, he would listen to the voice of God and write down the words that he heard. These prayer-poems nurtured his soul in the cold hard light of day.

Hope without risk is not hope,
which is believing in risky loving,
the blind leap, letting God take over.
I almost feel the need to shout — 'Be rash!'

Don't forget that boldness is a virtue —
More than a virtue — a gift of the Spirit of God.
No, do not give in.
Grace divine was your good beginning.
That grace is better which does not falter.
But the greatest is to keep going, however harassed, to the end.

Suggestions for Meditation:
» What aspect of this story did you relate to most?
» Which be-attitude do you feel Helder embodied best?
» What is the most valuable lesson you can learn from this story?

Remember Jesus said:
'In his hometown a prophet without honour.' *Matthew 13:57*
But 'my Father will honour the one who serves me.' *John 12:26*

PASTOR SON

The Man Who Adopted His Enemy

Pastor Son was the chaplain at a leprosarium called Ae-yang-won — the 'Garden of Loving Care' — near Yo-su in Korea. When Son was appointed to his post in 1940, about a thousand leprosy sufferers and their families were living there.

The Japanese had annexed Korea, and had embarked on a vigorous campaign to 'Japanise' the country. All Koreans were not only required to bow before the Japanese flag, but to take part in Shinto rituals that many felt were offensive to their Christian faith.

For a while, Pastor Son's quiet boycott of these requirements went unnoticed. But in due course, his refusal to go along with the program was reported to the authorities. He was arrested, brought before the court, charged with sedition, and sentenced to prison in Kwang-ju.

A Japanese was appointed in the pastor's place, and Son's wife and children were consequently displaced. So the family decided to follow Pastor Son and move to Pusan — close to the prison in Kwang-ju. The two older sons, Tong-in and Tong-sin, got work in a barrel factory to support the family. Tong-sin would secretly visit the leprosarium, encouraging the folks there to keep the faith.

In 1945, after the war was over and the Japanese had withdrawn from Korea, Pastor Son and his family were able to return to live with their beloved community of people with leprosy at Ae-yang-won. Tong-in and Tong-sin, the two older sons, who had taken on a lot of pastoral responsibility in the absence of their father, were more than happy to help him out in the community.

However, instead of living happily ever after, on 22 October 1948, both Tong-in and Tong-sin were caught in a communist uprising, and killed by some of the young communists.

Pastor Son was devastated. He had survived incarceration at the hands of the Japanese, only to live to see his two sons killed by his own people. So he decided to track down their killers. Pastor Son heard that one of the boys who had been involved in the killing had been arrested, and was about to be handed over for trial to the National Army who had occupied the town to restore order. So Pastor Son quickly dispatched Pastor Ra to talk to the boy on his behalf.

By the time Pastor Ra tracked down the suspect, he was already in army custody. So he approached the soldiers and asked them for permission to speak to their prisoner. He then introduced himself to the boy on the floor at their feet as the emissary of the victims' father, and asked if they might talk for a few minutes about the murders that had occurred. The prisoner said his name was Chai-sun. To begin with, he claimed that he knew about the murders, but had nothing to do with them himself. However, after talking for a while, he finally confessed that he had been part of the group who had shot Tong-in and Tong-sin.

> *'I thank God that he gave me the love to adopt as my son the enemy who killed my dear sons.'*
> — Pastor Son

It was then that Pastor Ra delivered Pastor Son's extraordinary message to the soldiers and their prisoner. 'Pastor Son has asked that the killer of his two sons should not be punished, but be forgiven, and be released into his custody — to be adopted in the place of the sons who were killed!'

Chai-sun could barely believe his ears. It seemed too good to be true. But he jumped at the chance. His parents begged the soldiers to let him go. And — eventually — they did so.

When Pastor Ra brought Chai-sun face to face with Pastor Son for the first time, the old pastor said to him: 'Don't worry. I have already forgiven you, and God is longing to forgive you too.'

Years later Chai-sun wrote to his adopted father, saying: 'Not because I want to gain heaven or to escape hell, but because of your love I have come to believe in Christ. And as your eldest son, I shall do everything I can to follow after my two brothers…in the footsteps of St Paul.'

Suggestions for Meditation:
» What aspect of this story did you relate to most?
» Which be-attitude do you feel Son embodied best?
» What is the most valuable lesson you can learn from this story?

Remember Jesus said:
'Sinners love those who love them…
But (I say) love your enemies and do good to them.' *Luke 6:32/35*

JACQUES ELLUL

The Prophet Of Bordeaux

Jacques Ellul was born on 6 January 1912 in Bordeaux, France. He was an only child. His father worked for local wine merchants and his mother taught art. He says his childhood was poor, but happy. He excelled at school, but never confined his study to books. After he finished his homework, Jacques would wander around the marshlands and the docks. It was a place he loved and was to live in for most of his life.

Jacques loved living in a cosmopolitan city and learning French, German, Latin and History in the local public school. He went on to study Law at the University of Bordeaux, where he encountered the writings of Karl Marx. He agreed with Marx's critique of society, but felt his views were inadequate to answer the great questions of life and death. Jacques turned to the Bible. He says: 'The Bible gave me more — establishing itself in my life at a different level than Marx's explanations.' As a result, he became a Christian in 1932.

At the university, Jacques joined a group of Protestant university students, and came across the writings of Karl Barth, 'the second great element in my intellectual life'. He was appointed lecturer at the University of Montpellier, then Strasbourg and Clermont-Ferrand. With his friend Bernard Charbonneau, Jacques developed his anarchistic Christian personalist philosophy.

With his wife Yvette, whom he married in 1937, Jacques had four children — three sons and a daughter.

During the war, the Germans arrested Jacques' father, and the German-controlled Vichy-French Government dismissed Jacques from his university post for anti-German comments he had made. Jacques' father died in custody and when the authorities came to arrest his wife Yvette, who had a British passport, Jacques took his family and fled to the countryside. There, in the little village of Martres, Jacques grew potatoes and corn to feed his family, and worked for the French Resistance, assisting Jews and others to escape the Nazis.

After the war, Jacques was appointed Professor of Law at the University of Bordeaux, and he shocked many of his colleagues by defending collaborators, whom he argued the French were now persecuting in exactly the same way that the Germans had persecuted him and his family. From 1944 to 1946, Jacques served as deputy mayor of the city of Bordeaux and, from 1946 to 1953, Jacques served on the National Synod of the Reformed Church of France. However, Jacques found these experiences so profoundly bitter and disturbing that he refused to be involved in party politics or institutional reform ever again.

> *'The Bible gave me more — establishing itself in my life at a different level than Marx's explanations.'*
> — Jacques Ellul

Jacques decided the best role for him to play in society was that of what we might call 'an engaged sage'. In the mornings, he would set time aside to pray, read and write. He wrote over fifty books and almost a thousand articles of major global intellectual significance, brilliantly critiquing the dominance of technology over spirituality, the tyranny of television, the role of propaganda, and the use of violence in modern societies. In the afternoons, Jacques would set time aside to receive visitors, pastor the house churches he was involved with, and supervise ministries to juvenile delinquents, drug addicts and homeless people in his own home town. The 'prophet of Bordeaux' was a model of praxis — or 'theory-in-practice'.

Jacques says that two soul friends — one an atheist and the other a Christian — sustained him in his ministry. His atheist friend kept him honest, exposing the hypocrisy of the Christianity he advocated; and his Christian friend gave him heart, by demonstrating the 'incredible authenticity' that he was called to.

Jacques Ellul died on 19 May 1994 in Bordeaux.

Jacques Ellul on Money

When Jacques Ellul was just eighteen years old, he read Karl Marx's *Das Kapital* and from then on regarded it as the most accurate analysis of the role of money in society that he had ever read. In his own book, *Money and Power*, Jacques Ellul argues that 'money is not neutral, something we can use as we like'. It is 'a powerful agent that sets itself against God's kingdom'. He cites the scripture which says that the 'love of money is the root of all evil'. He exposes the folly of a purely socio-economic approach — whether communism or capitalism — and argues for personal responsibility. According to him, the only way we can exorcise the demonic power of money in our lives is through the practice of generosity — living 'by the law of grace, not by the law of the marketplace'.

Suggestions for Meditation:
» What aspect of this story did you relate to most?
» Which be-attitude do you feel Jacques embodied best?
» What is the most valuable lesson you can learn from this story?

Remember Jesus said:
'You will know the truth, and the truth will set you free.' *John 8:32*

CLARENCE JORDAN

The Race-Mixing Communist

Clarence Jordan was born in 1912, and brought up in the state of Georgia in the deep south of the United States. He grew up in a Christian tradition which preached grace, but practised disgraceful prejudice.

The young Clarence couldn't abide this blatant misrepresentation of the gospel, and determined that he would find a way to flesh out the gospel more faithfully — a way that would reflect Christ's love for all people equally, black and white alike!

Clarence studied Agriculture at the University of Georgia, and the New Testament at the Southern Baptist Theological Seminary, where he came up with the idea of developing a working farm that would demonstrate such New Testament values as 'koinonia', or 'community'.

So, in 1942, long before the civil rights movement really got going, Clarence started Koinonia Farm, as his attempt to develop counter-cultural, multi-racial community slap bang in the middle of the Ku Klux Klan heartland!

Koinonia Farm was like nothing the locals had ever seen before. Clarence, and his wife Florence, and their friends invited both blacks and whites to join them, as equal partners, in their enterprise.

Private income was contributed to a common purse, and personal property was considered common wealth. So, right from the start, the locals referred to them as those 'race-mixing Communists!'

Clarence and Florence tried to explain that they were Christians, not Communists. But it was hard to convince anyone of this when most of the local Christians wanted nothing to do with them. Sunday after Sunday, the folk from Koinonia would turn up for worship at one local church or another, only to be turned away because the group from Koinonia were black and white, and, for the most part, local churches were 'For Whites Only'!

This made Clarence even more determined to confront the Churches with their hypocrisy. He began his own translation of the New Testament, setting the story of Jesus in the 20th Century, and staging the disputes Jesus had with the Pharisees and Sadducees between Jesus and the First Church of Gainsville in Georgia.

As the Chatanooga Times says, Clarence's Cotton Patch Version 'set off explosions in the mind'. In the Cotton Patch Version, Jesus calls his mission 'the God Movement', and explains that the purpose of the God Movement is 'to help those who have been grievously insulted to find dignity.' (Luke 4:19)

Jordan's Jesus confronts local Christians, saying, 'It will be hell for you, you phonies, because you tithe your pennies, nickles, and dimes, and pass up the more important things in the Bible, such as justice, sharing and integrity! You addle-brained leaders, you save your trading stamps, and throw your groceries in the garbage!' (Matt 23:23–24)

> *'It will be hell for you phonies, because you tithe your pennies, nickles, and dimes, and pass up the more important things in the Bible, such as justice.'*
> —Clarence

As you can imagine, the 'addle-brained leaders' were not amused with these remarks. So they organised a total boycott of Koinonia Farm. Local people were forbidden to sell Koinonia any farm supplies, or purchase any Koinonia farm products.

Christians from all over the country, who sympathised with what the folk on Koinonia Farm were trying to do, tried to break the boycott, by bringing in poultry feed and trucking out chickens and eggs.

The Klu Klux Klan then got in on the act, with drive-by shootings and dynamite bombings. But the folk on Koinonia Farm stood firm. They were pacifist and refused to fight fire with fire. But they were also steadfast and refused to be run out of town.

In spite of constant death threats, Clarence continued to affirm his faith in Christ and Christ's call to inclusive multi-ethnic community. When he died in 1969, Clarence was still one of the most hated men in his county, but he left us a legacy of tough love that we would do well to heed if we want to try to develop inclusive multi-ethnic communities in an increasingly racist society.

Suggestions for Meditation:
» What aspect of this story did you relate to most?
» Which be-attitude do you feel Clarence embodied best?
» What is the most valuable lesson you can learn from this story?

Remember Jesus said:
'He who hears my words and puts them into practice is like a person building a house, who dug down deep and laid the foundation on rock. When a flood came, the torrent struck that house but could not shake it, because it was well built.' *Luke 6:46–48*

JOSÉ MARIA ARIZMENDIARRIETA

The Co-op Priest

José Maria Arizmendiarrieta was born in 1915 on a farm about thirty miles from Mondragon. Being brought up in Basque country, José grew up Basque — gritty, proud and independent. Being brought up Catholic in Basque country meant José grew up Catholic Basque — well-grounded, well-educated and passionately progressive.

When he was thirteen José left his village and went to seminary. At seminary he immersed himself in progressive Catholic social teaching.

From 1936 to 1939, Spain was plunged into the Spanish Civil War. For the Basques, 'La Geurra Civil' was a battle for autonomy and democracy against tyranny. Most of the Basque clergy supported the Basque patriots.

José wrote patriotic articles for Eguna during the war. As a consequence José was arrested and imprisoned. He expected to be executed; but was given a reprieve, and was released.

In 1941, at the age of twenty-six, he was assigned as a priest to Mondragon, where he was to work for the rest of his life.

Because of his interest in social issues, José was assigned as a counsellor to 'Accion Catolica'. But there wasn't a lot of 'accion' in Mondragon at the time.

Unemployment was a major problem in Mondragon, so José tried to get more students enrolled in an apprentice training school run by a local steel company. The management blocked this move, so José set up a community-managed training school.

The self-financed, self-governed apprentice school, which José started in 1943, was a great success. In 1948, José organised the League of Education and Culture, which, in turn, developed a comprehensive educational program that now provides comprehensive community education to approximately forty-five thousand students.

This program, with its emphasis not only on technical, but also on ethical education, was the foundation upon which the Basques were able to build a remarkable co-operative movement.

In 1952, eleven students passed their engineering exams at the University of Zaragoza. In 1954, five of those students decided to buy a small bankrupt factory and turn it into a worker-controlled co-operative. By the end of 1958 the co-op had 149 employees.

Their success inspired a whole range of co-operative enterprises including large machine shops, appliance manufacturers, technical services, research and development organisations, a chain of department stores, and even a worker-controlled bank.

Today, there are now more than a hundred and seventy worker-owned-and-operated co-operatives, providing 21,000 workers with good jobs, serving over 100,000 people in Mondragon.

To begin with, the co-ops operated informally along democratic lines, but José knew that for them to be truly durable democratic organisations, they needed to develop formal democratic principles and procedures.

Fascist-influenced Spanish laws made this very difficult to do. So José spent a lot of his time finding ways for the co-ops to break with the old rules that governed corporate structures, and make new rules that would help them develop more innovative and more responsive participatory co-operative structures.

'Co-operation is the authentic integration of people in the economic and social process that shapes a new social order; the co-operators must make this objective extend to all those that hunger and thirst for justice in the working world.'
—José

José Maria Arizmendiarrieta died in 1976, but his legacy lives on in Mondragon as what many observers consider the best, practical, post-modern alternative to both capitalism and communism.

Suggestions for Meditation:
» What aspect of this story did you relate to most?
» Which be-attitude do you feel José Maria embodied best?
» What is the most valuable lesson you can learn from this story?

Remember Jesus said:
'The kingdom of heaven is like a mustard seed, which a man took and planted in his field. Though it is the smallest of all your seeds, yet when it grows, it is the largest of garden plants and becomes a tree, so that the birds of the air come and perch in its branches.'
Matthew 13:31–32

DESMOND TUTU

The Voice of the Voiceless

Desmond Tutu was born on 7 October 1931 in Klerksdorp, South Africa. His father was a teacher and his mother a domestic worker. They nurtured the young Desmond in a culture of respect that stood in stark contrast to the intolerant culture of the day. 'I never learnt to hate,' he said.

When he was twelve, Desmond moved with his family to Johannesburg. He attended Johannesburg Bantu High School and became a teacher with a set of skills he was to use effectively the rest of his life.

In 1955, Desmond married Leah, with whom he had four children. In 1957, Desmond decided to become a priest, and began his training for ordination the following year. Ordained in 1961, he became a chaplain at the University of Fort Hare, one of the only good-quality universities open to 'blacks' in South Africa. It served as a creative think-tank for the politics of dissent.

From 1962 to 1966, Desmond studied theology at King's College in England. While he was away, Nelson Mandela, and seven other leaders of the African National Congress (ANC), were tried for treason, convicted and sentenced to life imprisonment for trying to overthrow the government. On his return, Desmond resumed his post as chaplain at the University of Fort Hare, using his lectures at Federal Theological Seminary as an opportunity to reflect biblically on the 'black' struggle.

From 1972 to 1975, Desmond worked as an Associate Director in Theology for the World Council of Churches. Then, in 1975, Desmond was appointed the first 'black' Dean of St. Mary's Cathedral, Johannesburg. From this moment, Desmond began to emerge as an eloquent spiritual advocate for 'equal rights for all'.

In 1976, Soweto, a black township to the south-west of Johannesburg, erupted in protest when the students were forced to use Afrikaans in schools. Police retaliated with tear gas and gunfire. Weeks of boycotts, marches, counter-attacks and violent clashes around the country left more than 500 people dead, thousands arrested, and thousands more seeking refuge outside the country. In response, Desmond penned a brilliant open letter to the Prime Minister, John Vorster, that was to become a model for Christian resistance. That same year, Desmond became Bishop of Lesotho and, two years later, Secretary-

General of the South African Council of Churches — which gave him the opportunity to work with the churches against the regime. Desmond denounced apartheid as 'evil and unchristian', and called for the abolition of internal passport laws and the cessation of forced deportation of 'blacks' by 'white' authorities to so-called 'homelands'.

During this time, Desmond developed a reputation for being able to work for reconciliation by talking to people on both sides of the argument. The United Democratic Front (UDF) was formed, out of a coalition of more than 600 organisations, with more than 3 million members, Desmond becoming a leading spokesperson. 'God's dream is that all of us will realize we are family. In God's family there are no enemies,' he said over and over again. 'When we recognize our interdependence, and start to live as brothers and sisters, then we become fully human.'

In 1984, Desmond was awarded the Nobel Peace Prize in recognition of 'the courage shown by black South Africans in their use of peaceful methods in the struggle against apartheid. At the award presentation, the chairman of the Nobel Committee said: 'Some time ago, television enabled us to see this year's laureate in a suburb of Johannesburg. A massacre of the black population had just taken place — the camera showed mutilated human beings and crushed children's toys. Innocent people had been murdered. Women and children mortally wounded. But, after the police vehicles had driven away with their prisoners, Desmond Tutu stood and spoke to a bitter congregation: 'Do not hate,' he said. 'Let us choose the peaceful way to freedom'.

Desmond was installed as Bishop of Cape Town in 1986 — the first black leader of South Africa's 1.6 million Anglicans. As media restrictions strangled free speech and organisations like the UDF were effectively banned, Desmond used his position as a leader of a middle-of-the-road multi-racial church to increase his criticism of apartheid.

After a stroke in 1989, hard-line apartheid President P.W. Botha resigned, making way for a more moderate F.W. de Klerk to negotiate with Nelson Mandela the terms and conditions of his release. In 1990,

'God's dream is that all of us will realize that we are family, that we are made for togetherness. In God's family, there are no outsiders, no enemies. Black and white, rich and poor, gay and straight, Jew and Arab, Muslim and Christian, Hindu and Buddhist — all belong. —Desmond

Mandela was freed and restrictions on banned organisations like the ANC were rescinded. In 1991, a National Peace Accord was signed, and nearly a thousand political prisoners were released. In 1992, an overwhelming majority of white South Africans voted *yes* for change in a national referendum. A 'Government of National Unity' was set up to facilitate a transition to democracy and, in 1994, Mandela was elected President.

In 1995, Desmond was asked to chair a Truth and Reconciliation Commission that would 'investigate human rights abuses and political crimes committed by both supporters and opponents of apartheid between 1960 and 10 May 1994'. The Commission was empowered to 'consider amnesty for those who confess their participation in atrocities and recommend compensation to survivors and their dependants'. Desmond said at the time: 'I hope by opening wounds to cleanse them, and stop them from festering.'

In 1996, Desmond retired as Archbishop to devote himself to his work on the Commission. As chair of the Commission, he heard 20,000 testimonials and received nearly 4,000 applications for amnesty. He said: 'We witnessed the ability of victims to forgive their torturers, and of former torturers to transform their lives.' The Commission has become an extraordinarily compelling example of how a nation can process the pain it has experienced through injustice without doing injustice in return.

Since he stepped down from the Commission, Desmond has set up his own Peace Trust, become a patron of the Sabeel Center for Peace in Jerusalem, and continued to be 'a voice for the voiceless' in challenging everyone from Robert Mugabe, President of Zimbabwe, to Thabo Mbeki, current President of South Africa. Nelson Mandela says of Desmond Tutu: 'Sometimes strident, often tender, never afraid and seldom without humour, Desmond Tutu's voice will always be 'the voice of the voiceless.'

Suggestions for Meditation:
» What aspect of this story did you relate to most?
» Which be-attitude do you feel Desmond embodied best?
» What is the most valuable lesson you can learn from this story?

Remember Jesus said:
'I have set you an example
that you should do as I have done.' *John 13:15*

GLADYS STAINES

A Widow Shows The Way Forward

Gladys Staines was born in 1951. She grew up at Peaks Crossing, just outside of Ipswich, in South-East Queensland. She was brought up in Brethren circles and became a devout Christian. After school, Gladys studied nursing in Ipswich and then completed her midwifery in Launceston.

Gladys met her husband Graham on a visit to India in 1981. Graham, a fellow Aussie, had gone to India to work with the poor — particularly people with leprosy. Gladys says that she was really impressed by his love for the people and felt that, in Graham, she had found the life-partner she was looking for. They were married in 1983, and had three children — one daughter, Esther, and two sons, Philip and Timothy.

When they were married, Gladys joined Graham in the management of the Leprosy Home in Baripada, Orissa. The Home not only provided treatment to leprosy patients, but also rehabilitation training in hand-weaving and in making *sabai* grass products. It also had its own dairy farm.

Gladys says that the Home had a good relationship with the people in the town of Baripada. When they fell sick, or were bitten by snakes, the townspeople often relied on the Staines to arrange their treatment.

Graham was fluent in the Oriya, Santhali and Ho languages — assisting in the translation of the Bible into the Ho language. When the children were born, Gladys made sure they learnt to speak the local language and played with the local kids — including the children of leprosy patients at the Baripada Leprosy Home.

Swami Agnivesh, a famous Arya Samaj Hindu leader, says: 'It is a mark of the Staines family's total identification with the local people that they could speak Santhali. What a refreshing contrast to the ways of our elite, who are eager to leave this country. Unlike the Staines family, they disdain to speak local languages. And it is anybody's guess if they would allow their children to play with the children of leprosy patients!'

Graham used to organize *'jungle'* camps for Christians in remote areas (*'jungli'* is Hindi for *'wild'*). On these camps, Graham would give Bible studies, and his colleagues would take sessions on health and hygiene. It was at the 14th annual jungle Bible camp in the village of

REFERENCES

Telemachus

C. Colson, *Loving God* (London: Hodder and Stoughton, 1983), pp. 268–269.

K.S. Latourette, *A History Of Christianity*, Vol 1 (New York: Harper & Row, 1975).

Nicholas

A. Jones, *The Wordsworth Dictionary Of Saints* (Ware: Chambers, W7R, 1992).

W. M. Zoba, 'The Evolution Of St. Nick', *Christianity Today*, 4 Dec 2000, p.44.

Martin of Tours

K. S. Latourette, *A History Of Christianity* Vol 1, 230ff, (New York: Harper & Row, 1975).

B. Shields, *Sharing The Good News God's Way* (Bruce T. Shields, 1998), p.89.

St Martin of Tours, http://www.catholic.org/saints/saint.php?saint_id=81

Basil of Caesarea

K.S. Latourette, *A History Of Christianity* (New York: Harper & Row, 1975).

The History of Christianity, (Berkhamsted: Lion, 1977).

http://en.wikipedia.org/wiki/Basil_the_Great#Life

http://www.catholic.org/saints/saint.php?saint_id=261

http://www.catholic-forum.com/saints/saintb05.htm (quote)

Patrick

Thomas Cahill, *How the Irish Saved Civilization* (New York: Doubleday, 1995).

Anita McSorely, *The St. Patrick You Never Knew* (St. Anthony Messenger, March 1997).

Bruce Shields, *Sharing The Good News God's Way* (Bruce T. Shields, 1998).

http://en.wikipedia.org/wiki/Saint_Patrick

http://www.americancatholic.org/Messenger/Mar1997/feature1.asp

Benedict

Jane Michele McClure, *The Rule of St Benedict*, http://www.thedome.org/AboutUs/rule.html

Saint Benedict of Nursia, http://www.osb.org/gen/bendct.html

St Benedict And His Order, http://www.christdesert.org/noframes/scholar/benedict/benedict_history.html

The Rule of St Benedict, http://en.wikipedia.org/wiki/Rule_of_St_Benedict#Secular_significance

Aidan

Bede, *A History Of The English Church And People* (Harmondsworth: Penguin 1955), pp. 145–165.

Aidan, http://www.catholic-forum.com/SAINTS/sainta24.htm

Lindisfarne: The Holy Isle, http://www.roca.org/OA/57/57e.htm

Saint Aidan, ed. from E.C.S. Gibson's *Northumbrian Saints* (1884). http://www.britannia.com/bios/saints/aidan.html

Wenceslaus

B. Adams, *Good King Wenceslas,* Fusion.

http://en.wikipedia.org/wiki/Saint_Wenceslas

Hugh of Lincoln

B. Eccleston, 'Hugh of Lincoln', *The Radical Tradition* (London: Darton, Longman & Todd, 1992).

J. Moses, 'Hugh of Lincoln — A Saint for Today' (St Hugh's Inala, 16 November 1986).

Francis of Assisi

R. Clouse, 'Francis of Assisi', *The History Of Christianity* (Berkhamsted: Lion, 1977).

R. Foster, *Streams of Living Water* (San Francisco: Harper, 1998).

R. Rohr 'A Life Pure And Simple', *Sojourners,* December 1981.

Elisabeth of Thuringia

J.R. Saul, *On Equilibrium,* 2001.

'Elisabeth of Many Castles', Christian History Institute, http://chi.gospelcom.net/GLIMPSEF/Glimpses/glmps131.shtml

Nilus Sorsky

Miles (Nilus) Stryker, 'Nilus of Sora — A Voice in the Wilderness', http://www.iocc.org/orthodoxdiakonia/index.php?id=10

'Nilus of Sora', http://www.orthodoxwiki.org/Nilus_of_Sora

Menno Simons

W. Estep, *The Anabaptist Story* (Grand Rapids: Eerdmans, 1963).

J. Roth, 'What Christians could learn from Menno Simons...' *Christianity Today,* 7 October 1996.

L. Verduin, *The Reformers and Their Stepchildren* (Grand Rapids: Eerdmans, 1964).

George Fox

Rufus Jones, 'An abstract of the life of George Fox' based on
George Fox – Seeker and Friend (New York & London: Harper & Bros. 1930).

http://www.gwyneddfriends.org/fox.htm

Bill Samuel, *The Beginnings of Quakerism*,
originally published 12 July 1998, at Suite101.com

http://www.quakerinfo.com/quakhist.shtml

Leonard Ravenhill, *George Fox – The unshakable Shaker*,
http://www.ravenhill.org/fox.htm

'Quakers: Fox and Penn's Holy Experiment',
http://www.san.beck.org/GPJ14-Quakers.html

Nikolaus Ludwig

J. Clark, 'Count Nicholas Ludwig von Zinzendorf', *The Ambassador*, 2000.

A Lion Handbook, *The History Of Christianity* (Oxford: Lion, 1977).

A Lion Book, *Heritage Of Freedom* (Oxford: Lion, 1984).

John Wesley

H. Snyder, *The Problem Of Wineskins* (Downers Grove: IVP, 1976).

H Snyder *The Radical Wesley* (Downers Grove: IVP, 1980).

Charles Finney

W. Cochran, *Charles Grandison Finney*, Memorial Address, Oberlin, 21 June 1908.

D. Dayton, *Discovering An Evangelical Heritage* (New York: Harper & Row, 1976).

Sojourner Truth

Sojourner Truth (Isabella Baumfree), www.lkwdpl.org/wihohio/trut-soj.htm

Sojourner Truth Ain't I A Woman?, www.webcom.com/-duane/truth.html

Caroline Chisholm

S. De Vries, 'The Immigrants' Friend', *Strength Of Spirit* (Alexandria: Millennium Books, 1995), pp. 91–110.

D. Northcroft, *Yarns On Women Pioneers* (Wallington: R.E. Press, 1944).

Te Whiti

Virginia Winder, *Conflict and Protest – Pacifist of Parihaka – Te Whiti o Rongomai* (Puke Ariki, 2003).

D. Scott, *Ask That Mountain* (Auckland: Reed, 1975).

Florence Nightingale

D. Felder, *The Giant Books Of Influential Women* (Sydney: The Book Co., 1997).

E. Hayes, *More Yarns on Christian Pioneers*
(Wallington: The Religious Education Press, 1959).

Henri Dunant

D. Neff, 'Compassionate in War, Christian in Vision', Posted 17 December 2004, http://www.icrc.org/

http://www.wcredcross.org/general/henry.html

Joseph de Veuster (Damien the Leper)

The Franciscans of St Anthony's Guild, *Damien The Leper* (New Jersey, 1974).

Mary MacKillop

D.H. Farmer, *Oxford Dictionary Of Saints*.

Female Firebrands And Reformers, www.geocities.com/eschiva.mckillop.html

Mary MacKillop, www.abc.net.au/btn/australians/mackillo.htm/

Mary MacKillop and the Sisters Of St. Joseph of the Sacred Heart,
www.sosj.org.au/NewSite/PeopleSection/HistoryPage.htm

John Gribble

John Gribble, *Black And Comely* (London: Morgan & Scott, 1884).

John Harris, *One Blood* (Sutherland: Albatross Books, 1990).

H. Reynolds, *This Whispering In Our Hearts* (St Leonards: Allen & Unwin, 1998).

Pandita Ramabai

J.N. Farquhar, *Modern Religious Movements In India* (New York: Macmillan, 1919).

John Foster, 'The First Woman In India's Public Life', *Men Of Vision*
(London: SCM, 1967) pp. 94–96.

C.F. Andrews

C.F. Andrews, *What I Owe To Christ* (London: 1932, 1970).

I.D.L. Clark, *C.F. Andrews Deenabandhu* (Calcutta: ISPCK, 1970).

David Gracie, *Gandhi and Charlie: The Story of a Friendship*
(Cambridge, MA: Cowley Publications, 1989).

Helen Keller

'Anne Sullivan', *In Search Of The Heroes*, graceproducts.com

'Helen Keller', *In Search Of The Heroes*, graceproducts.com

Toyohiko Kagawa

W, Axling, *Kagawa* (London: SCM, 1932).

Schildgen, *Toyohiko Kagawa* (Berkeley: Centenary Books, 1988).

Dorothy Day

James Forest, 'A Biography Of Dorothy Day', in *The Encyclopedia of American Catholic History,* ed. Michael Glazier and Thomas J. Shelley (The Liturgical Press, 2003).

Michael True, *Justice Seekers, Peace Makers* (Mystic: Twenty-Third Publications, 1985).

B. Randall, 'Dorothy Day', *Illuminating Lives,* 1996, www.mcs.drexel.edu/~gbrandal/Illum_html/Day.html

Dietrich Bonhoeffer

Dietrich Bonhoeffer, *Voices In The Night,* ed. Edwin Robertson (Grand Rapids: Zondervan, 1999).

Simone Weil

Dorothee Soelle, *Suffering* (Philadelphia: Fortress Press, 1975).

Simone Weil, *Waiting On God* (Glasgow: Collins, 1951).

Dom Helder Camara

H. Camara, *The Desert Is Fertile* (London: Sheed & Ward, 1978).

H. Camara, *A Thousand Reasons For Living* (London, D. L.T, 1981).

B. Lecumberri, *Brazil's Helder Camara, Champion Of The Poor, Dies at 90,* Agence France Press, Saturday 28 August 1999.

Pastor Son

Y.C. Ahn, *The Seed Must Die* (Kingswood: IVF, 1965).

Jacques Ellul

P. Chastenet, *A Short Biography of Jacques Ellul,* www.ellul.org/bio_e.htm trans. by Lesley Graham.

Clarence Jordan

D. Lee, 'Clarence Jordan: A Biographical Sketch', *The Universe Bends Towards Justice.*

José Maria Arizmendiarrieta

Roy Morrison, *We Build The Road As We Travel* (Philadelphia PA: New Society Publishers, 1991).

Albert Luthuli

C. Davey, *50 Lives For God* (London: Oliphants, 1973).

Albert Luthuli, *Let My People Go* (London: Collins, 1962).

Article by Prof. Kader Asmal, MP, Minister of Education, on Albert Luthuli, for the *Financial Mail*, fmmail@tml.co.za

Desmond Tutu

Bruce Harris, *Desmond Tutu*, www.moreorless.au.com

Desmond Tutu, The Rainbow People of God (London: Bantam, 1995).

Desmond Tutu's Recipe For Peace, www.beliefnet.com/story/

Gladys Staines

Swami Agnivesh, *Healing The Spirit Of Gladys Staines*, www.swamiagnivesh.com

S. David and Manpreet Singh, 'Once You Forgive, There Will Be Healing', *Christianity Today*, February 2003.

www.ingramcontent.com/pod-product-compliance
Lightning Source LLC
Chambersburg PA
CBHW080550170426
43195CB00016B/2740